Churches
and Abbeys
of Scotland

Martin Coventry
Joyce Miller

GOBLINSHEAD
Musselburgh

Churches and Abbeys of Scotland

First published 2003

© Martin Coventry & Joyce Miller 2003

Developed, updated and expanded from
Wee Guide to Old Churches and Abbeys of Scotland
© *Martin Coventry & Joyce Miller 1997*

Published by GOBLINSHEAD
130B Inveresk Road, Musselburgh EH21 7AY
Tel: 0131 665 2894; fax: 0131 653 6566
Email: goblinshead@sol.co.uk

British Library Cataloguing in Publication Data
A catalogue record for this book is available from
the British Library.

ISBN 1 899874 29 1

Printed by Polestar AUP, Aberdeen, Scotland

**If you would like a colour catalogue of our
publications please contact:
Goblinshead, 130B Inver esk Road,
Musselbur gh EH21 7A Y, Scotland, UK.**

Contents

How to use this book

The introduction (pages 1-15) is an overview of Christianity in Scotland, followed by more than 200 churches, abbeys, chapels, crosses and other monuments to visit (pages 18-103). A map (pages 16-17) locates each site. Each entry begins with the name of the church or site, whether it is in the care of Historic Scotland (HS) or The National Trust for Scotland (NTS), its map number in square ([204 (H4)]) brackets with the grid reference on the map, location, and then its National Grid Reference and OS Landranger number. This is followed by a description of the site, facilities, access and opening, and contact details.

There is information on saints (pages 104-113); a description of the different monastic and other orders (pages 114-115), and a glossary of terms (pages 116-118) includes a simple plan layout of an abbey, collegiate church, cathedral and parish church.

An index (pages 119-122) lists all the sites (both by name and location), people and events alphabetically. Bold entries refer to sites listed in the main part of the book, bold page numbers refer to this entry, and underlined page numbers refer to an illustration. Many churches are listed under their dedication: if this is the case, the site has also been indexed by the city, town or location.

Selected further reading

Cowan, Ian B. and D. E. Easson *Medieval Religious Houses: Scotland*, London, 1986

Donaldson, Gordon *Scottish Church History*, Edinburgh, 1985

Fawcett, Richard *Scottish Abbeys and Priories*, London, 1994

Fawcett, Richard *Scottish Cathedrals*, London, 1997

Fawcett, Richard *Scottish Medieval Churches*, Edinburgh, 1985

Forrester, Duncan and Douglas Murray (eds.) *Studies in the History of Worship in Scotland*, Edinburgh, 1984

Jones, Alison *The Wordsworth Dictionary of Saints*, Ware, 1994

McKean, Charles (ed.) *Illustrated Architectural Guides*, Edinburgh *Series of books covering most of Scotland*

New, Anthony *A Guide to the Abbeys of Scotland*, London, 1988

Salter, Mike *The Old Parish Churches of Scotland*, Malvern, 1994

Scotland's Churches Scheme *Churches to Visit in Scotland*, Edinburgh

Towill, Edwin Sprott *Saints of Scotland*, Edinburgh, 1983

Note

Hundreds of fine sites are in the care of Historic Scotland, including abbeys, cathedrals, collegiate churches, chapels and other monuments. If it is intended to visit many of these, consider joining Historic Scotland, as, along with other benefits, entry to properties is free for members.

Historic Scotland
Longmore House, Salisbury Place, Edinburgh EH9 1SH
Tel: 0131 668 8800 Fax: 0131 668 8888
Email: hs.explorer@scotland.gsi.gov.uk
Web: www.historic-scotland.gov.uk

Preface

Thistle Guides are intended to be both portable and detailed, delivering a considerable amount of information on a topic in a handy, compact format. Many of Scotland's best places to visit are included with enough history and background to make every visit as worthwhile as possible.

This first volume lists many of the most interesting, impressive, picturesque or important churches, abbeys, crosses and other monuments, from the beginning of the Christian period until the Reformation and beyond. We have included 200 sites, both complete, altered and ruinous: from great cathedrals and abbeys through collegiate and parish churches to smaller chapels, caves, wells and carved crosses. It has, however, been difficult to limit the number of entries to 200, and we have attempted to include as wide a selection and type of places as possible, inevitably leading to the exclusion of many fine sites.

Although this is a small book (at least in format), it does contain a lot of information and, while we have tried to check everything, mistakes or omissions may have occurred. Please contact us if you think it could be improved or we have been remiss in not including any sites.

Many thanks to everyone who helped with the book, including Doug Houghton for the cover photograph of St Magnus Cathedral, Kirkwall, and Burntisland Parish Church and Dalmeny Parish Church for their photos. The back cover photographs are of Iona Abbey, MacMillan's Cross at Kilmory Knap, the Church of the Holy Rude in Stirling, and St Rule's Tower and St Andrews Cathedral.

MC & JM, Musselburgh, January 2003

Top left: Arbroath Abbey
Above: Dunfermline Abbey
Left: St Ninian's Chapel, Isle of Whithorn
Bottom left: Church of the Holy Rude
Below: Kilchoman Cross

Introduction

The story of religion and worship in Scotland is as old as the people themselves, although what form this took in ancient times is speculative. Numerous standing stones, henges, stone circles and burial cairns can be found all over the country, but the beliefs that shaped their construction have been lost. Later generations developed rituals and uses for these stones of their own, including healing and magic – to cure toothache or enhance fertility: practices which would be condemned by the Reformed church in the 16th century. Springs and wells had always had significance, and it seems likely that these were visited for healing and good luck long before the advent of Christianity.

EARLY CHRISTIAN WORSHIP – SAINTS AND LEGENDS

By the time of the Roman invasion of Britain, 79 to 84 AD, written accounts record that the inhabitants of these islands were Druids. Although some of the Roman invaders of Britain were Christian, they appear to have made little attempt to introduce Christianity to the general population.

This was left to Ninian in 430 AD, after the Roman legions had been recalled, and Palladius about the same time. Ninian had been educated at Rome, was a disciple of St Martin of Tours, and founded a religious house at Whithorn – *Candida Casa*. This was organised into cells, for the monks; agricultural work to provide food; and evangelistic work to convert pagans to Christianity. There were

Whithorn Priory – built on the site of Ninian's Candida Casa

Introduction

three sites at Whithorn: the diocesan centre at *Candida Casa*; the monastery at Isle of Whithorn; and a hermitage at Physgill, now known as St Ninian's Cave. Many of these early Christian sites have springs or wells, and it may be that these were pre-Christian sacred sites.

Somewhat later, missionaries travelled from Ireland to the west of Scotland, including Brendan, Moluag and Maelrubha, setting up monasteries at places such as Lismore and Applecross. In 563 Columba settled on Iona, which may have been a Druidical site and became an important centre of Celtic Christianity. Like Ninian, Columba combined monasticism and missionary work. More is known about Columba than many of his contemporaries because of the work of Adamnan, who wrote the *Vita Sancti Columbae* in which he included many miraculous stories. Mungo, whose actual name was Kentigern, was active in the west of Scotland, his shrine is in the crypt of Glasgow Cathedral. Other saints, such as

Glasgow Cathedral: Mungo is believed to have been buried in the crypt

Ternan and Serf were making (or had made) missions to the heart, north and east of Scotland.

Parting of the Ways – Roman Versus Celtic Christianity

In the 7th century, Aidan, a missionary from Iona, spread Christianity to Northumberland, establishing Lindisfarne, Melrose and Coldingham as Christian monasteries. His work was continued by Cuthbert, who had been a novice at Melrose.

Cuthbert eventually became prior, and later bishop, of Lindisfarne, but also took time to live as a hermit on St Cuthbert's Isle and the Farne Islands. During his time as prior of Lindisfarne, the practices of the Celtic and Roman forms of worship were debated at the Synod of Whitby in 664. The differences between the two forms included the dating of Easter, and the necessity of tonsure, but the fundamental argument was between Episcopal (bishoprics) and monastic organisation.

In Celtic monastic organisation a bishop was subordinate to an abbot, but with an Episcopal organisation bishops were head of, and superior to, all in a diocesan area. The Roman form of organisation was accepted, although Colman, who had represented the Celtic argument at Whitby, and others returned to Iona where they maintained an independent organisation until 716.

Another major site of religious settlement was St Andrews where Rule had established a monastery– the site later occupied by the Cathedral. In 733 Acca, Bishop of Hexham, brought the relics of St Andrew to Fife. Lindisfarne, Iona and St Andrews became centres for Christian stone carving, and the magnificent crosses of Kildalton and Iona date from around this time, while the cross at Ruthwell dates from the 7th century.

In 793 the main coastal religious sites of Iona and Lindisfarne suffered the first of several attacks by the Vikings. In 806, 68 monks were reputedly slaughtered. Iona was abandoned in 826, and some of the community – with Kenneth MacAlpin's encouragement – moved to the safer location of Dunkeld. A carved wooden box, decorated with bronze and semi-precious stones, known as the Monymusk Reliquary or the *Breccbennach* was said to have contained a relic of bone from Columba. It is now in the Museum of Scotland. The manuscript, inscribed on Iona, which would later be known as the *Book of Kells* was taken to Kells, County Meath in Ireland. Cuthbert's relics were translated from Lindisfarne to Durham.

With the removal from Iona, the Irish and Scottish Churches became increasingly separate. Dunkeld was for a time regarded as the centre of the Scottish Church, but was eventually replaced by St Andrews. The bishops of St Andrews were known as *Episcopus Scottorum* – chief bishop of Scotland, but were not granted archbishopric status by Rome. This became a serious problem during the wars with England in the 13th and 14th centuries, as the English Church – as well as Edward I – claimed superiority over their northern neighbour.

MONKS AND MONASTERIES – THE ARRIVAL OF RELIGIOUS ORDERS
During the reign of Malcolm Canmore, his queen, Margaret, was very involved with both the secular and religious trends of the period, and was critical of what

she saw as laxness in Church organisation, including the lack of diocesan structure.

She founded a Benedictine abbey at Dunfermline in 1072, and revived the monastery on Iona. More importantly she laid the foundations of Church reform that her son David would continue. Margaret herself was reported – by her devoted biographer Turgot – to have been a pious and practical Christian. She provided care for the poor, notably a ferry to cross the Firth

Dunfermline Abbey – founded by St Margaret

of Forth for those undertaking pilgrimage to Dunfermline and St Andrews. Margaret was canonised in 1250, and her chapel in Edinburgh Castle was built by her son, David.

In Ireland as early as the 8th century *Keledei, Celi De* or *Culdees* – friends of God – set up isolated religious communities. Several of these arrived in Scotland and set up monasteries at Abernethy, Brechin, Loch Leven and Monifieth, as well as St Andrews and elsewhere. Although Margaret had respect for the piety of these communities, their independence was gradually eroded as they became incorporated into, or replaced by, continental forms of monasticism.

David I continued his mother's reforms in a number of ways, both at parish and higher level. In order to provide for a church and priest in every parish, teinds or tithes – a payment of 10% of annual income – were introduced. He organised and divided the kingdom into 10 bishoprics, although there were actually 13 within the boundaries of modern Scotland, re-establishing old dioceses and introducing a new one in Caithness. Galloway remained under the control of York. The dioceses of Orkney and Sodor – the Western Isles – were under Norwegian rule, the Archbishopric of Nidaros or Trondheim: Sodor until the late 13th century, and Orkney until 1383.

The dioceses which were re-introduced by David, and his heir Alexander I, all had cathedrals (although some of them later): Dunblane, Glasgow, Aberdeen, Brechin, Dunkeld, Elgin, Fortrose, St Andrews, Whithorn and Dornoch. Whithorn and St Andrews were monastic, and had priories attached, while the others had secular canons.

ORDER AND DESIGN – DAILY ROUTINE AND RITUAL

The daily order and life of the religious houses was strictly controlled and based on Roman rite, although local variations were introduced by way of dedications to native saints, particularly in the 15th century. There were usually seven services per day, with the high mass being the main celebration.

The architectural plan of medieval cathedrals was fairly standard. The main area – the choir and presbytery – was for the celebration of the religious services by the clergy; but there was an area – the nave – for lay people to congregate and observe at least some of the major festivals.

The main axis (for all churches) was east to west, and the high altar was at the east end. An area, near the altar – called the choir – was where the canons were positioned during the service; and the lay congregation remained in the west end – the nave. There were sometimes projecting wings, at right angles – transepts – in which there were smaller altars to saints. The presbytery, at the east end of the choir, held the bishop's throne and stalls for the canons and other important people. The nave and choir were separated by a screen – a rood screen – often highly carved, the finest surviving example is in Glasgow Cathedral.

Glasgow and Kirkwall are the only two cathedrals which survived the Reformation intact. Brechin, Dunblane, Dunkeld, Dornoch, Iona, Lismore, and Aberdeen continue to be used as parish churches, and have been repaired, re-modelled and sympathetically (at least latterly) restored as needed. Elgin, Fortrose, St Andrews, and Whithorn are ruinous.

David I founded many houses of continental religious orders. The Benedictines had been introduced by Margaret. David introduced Cluniac Benedictines at Newcastle and Crossraguel, and Cistercians at Melrose in 1136. He also founded a house of Tironensian canons at Selkirk in 1113, although it later moved to Kelso.

It was not only the Crown which introduced religious orders to Scotland. The Valliscaulians Order was introduced at Ardchattan by Duncan MacDougall, Lord Lorne in 1230. Alexander I, David I's brother, had founded an order of Augustinian canons at Scone in 1120, which spread to many houses including Cambuskenneth, Inchcolm, Loch Leven and St Andrews. The Premonstratensian order of canons was introduced at Dryburgh, again by David, and there were eventually six houses, including Whithorn. There were also Trinitarian houses, including one at Peebles.

Introduction

David I introduced Anglo-Norman building style with its Romanesque features of rounded arches and windows. The overall pattern was more squared and squat to provide the stability and support for heavy walls and vaulted stone ceilings. Chevron – zigzag – ornamentation over door arches is a distinct Norman feature. Good examples of Romanesque design can be seen at Dalmeny, Leuchars, St Margaret's Chapel in Edinburgh Castle, and the Abbey church at Dunfermline.

In the mid to late 12th century, Gothic style of architecture was introduced. With improved building techniques, such as buttressing, this style allowed for more decorative, lighter designs. The use of pointed arches and windows meant there could be both more, and larger, windows decorated with tracery. Vaults were higher with concave arches.

By the 13th century, other orders had been founded in Europe in reaction to the excesses of wealth and ornamentation to which some in the Church were prone. These begging, or mendicant orders, were founded by St Francis and St Dominic, and located their orders near towns in order to preach to the laity. These orders, the Dominicans – Blackfriars – and Franciscans – Greyfriars – reached Scotland about 1230, and set up friaries around towns such as Edinburgh, Perth, St Andrews, Dundee, Glasgow, Montrose, Ayr, Dumfries, Inverness and many others. Because these orders had their establishments in towns, few of the Friary buildings remain standing: many were singled out for destruction at the Reformation.

Monastic life was standardised. The religious day was much like cathedral worship with eight services or 'hours' on ordinary days. As monastic communities grew, there was an increased number and variety of special roles for the monks – cooks, gardeners, care of the sick, music, the writing of manuscripts, as well as the administration and overseeing of the large amounts of feudal lands which the monasteries held. Many establishments also had lay-brothers, who assisted in the more menial tasks around the abbey.

The plan of monastic churches was similar to the cathedrals, and they were located on the north side of the cloister. The other monastic buildings – the domestic buildings – were located to the south side of the church, forming a rectangle known as a cloister. These included the refectory, the dormitory and the chapter house. Often there would be a passageway and stairs leading from the dormitory into the church, so the monks did not have to go outside when they attended services at night. There would also be a parlour; warming room; kitchen; infirmary; cellars as well as accommodation for lay-brothers; guest accommodation; store-rooms; bake-houses and brew-houses.

The best-preserved complex of domestic buildings can be found at Inchcolm, while substantial parts of the church can been seen at Jedburgh and Melrose.

Arbroath Abbey – founded in memory of Thomas a Becket

The nave at Dunfermline Abbey continued to be used as a parish church after the Reformation, but the remains of the domestic buildings, like Dryburgh and Melrose, give an impression of the size and layout.

The Tironensian abbey at Arbroath was founded by William the Lion in 1178, and although it is ruinous, is of significance because of its contribution during the Wars on Independence. In 1320 a letter was sent to Pope John XXII, drafted by Abbot Bernard de Linton of Arbroath. This letter, which would later be known as the *Declaration of Arbroath,* complained about the repeated harassment of the Scots by the English. The Scottish Church was determined to remain independent. There are the remains of many other fine abbeys in Scotland, and the abbey at Pluscarden has been rebuilt and is now occupied by the Benedictine Order.

The majority of the population, however, did not worship in such buildings. Small simple rectangular churches, divided into chancel and nave, often with a thatched roof, were commonplace in small or rural parishes.

RELATIONSHIP WITH ROME – NATIONAL AND INTERNATIONAL TRENDS

Surviving liturgies from the 13th to 16th centuries show that the form of service worshipped in Scotland did not vary much from the Roman ritual. The *filia specialis* relationship which had been granted by Rome, after the Wars of Independence, had removed any attempt at Episcopal interference by York and established a direct relationship with Rome. But no Scottish archbishopric had been created, and with the wars and after there was increased deviation between the two.

Introduction

It was during the 15th century that Scotland was granted two archbishoprics: St Andrews in 1472, and Glasgow in 1492. In the same century, other continental trends in religious worship found popularity in Scotland: new cults such as Holy Blood; the Passion; the Five Wounds; while there was also an increase in dedications and re-dedications to native Scottish saints.

Pilgrimage to sites in Spain and Italy were popular, but there were also major sites in Scotland. Originally native saints had been worshipped at local shrines, but some relics were moved and relocated to larger churches or cathedrals, or larger churches were built for them. These included St Machar at Aberdeen, St Mungo or Kentigern at Glasgow, St Duthac at Tain, St Mirren at Paisley, and St Ninian at Whithorn.

Not only were the relics of local saints venerated, but the liturgies and services held introduced new feasts and ceremonies into the religious calendar. There are surviving breviaries from this time which show that there were numerous feast days for Scottish, Irish or Northumbrian saints, as well as other major saints' days. The breviary from Fowlis Easter includes seven Scottish saints, and the *Arbuthnott Missal* six (this was compiled at St Ternan's Church at Arbuthnott).

By the time of Bishop Elphinstone – Bishop of Aberdeen between 1483-1514 – the yearly liturgy was so overcrowded and disorganised that he commissioned a new *Aberdeen Breviary*, which he intended would become the national calendar. English material was removed – except for Northumbrian saints – and the ceremonies were standardised. His attempt

St Andrews Cathedral – now a fine ruin

to unify national worship was not successful, however, as, by the time his breviary was printed, Rome had brought out a new standard: the Quinonez breviary. There is a list of some of the saints to which dedications were made towards the end of the book.

Apart from the official church worship conducted by clerics, there was an increasing fashion for personal piety in the 15th and 16th centuries. As mentioned, cults such as the Holy Blood and the Rosary became popular, as did dedicating altars and collegiate churches to favourite or patron saints. These were institutions in which a number of secular clergy were provided for by an endowment, but the clergy administered themselves. The purpose of the college was to ensure the saying of prayers and masses for the dead in perpetuity: they were also considerably less costly to create and maintain than priories or abbeys.

Many of these churches were founded in rural areas, near the lands or household of the lay patron. Some of the early colleges had royal patronage, but the majority were provided for by wealthy magnates. Others were located in towns, and were provided for by their councils. These buildings were all built to unique plans, and became increasingly ornate, as they became symbols of status and wealth.

Some fine examples remain at Rosslyn, Seton, Restalrig, Chapel Royal and the Holy Rude at Stirling, Dunglass, Lincluden, Bothwell, Cullen and Innerpeffray. Many of these churches had aisled naves and transepts, and were built in a cruciform shape.

Rejection of Rome – Reforming Ideas

At the same time, new Reforming ideas arrived in Scotland from the Continent and England. The Roman Church was denounced as corrupt, morally and spiritually, and despite attempts at reform from within both within Scotland and by the Papacy, the ideas of Calvin and Luther found support and following, particularly in areas like Perth, Dundee and Edinburgh.

Although there were some individuals executed as martyrs – Patrick Hamilton was burnt in 1528 and George Wishart was burnt by Cardinal Beaton in 1546 – the Reformation in Scotland was remarkable for its relative lack of violence. In 1557 the *First Bond* was signed by several earls and lords, which declared their intention to overthrow the Roman Church.

There were episodes of open hostility, and many friaries, abbeys and churches were damaged or destroyed. The Reformers eventually achieved their goal when Scotland was declared a Protestant country in 1560, and abbeys and priories were dissolved, their land and property going to the Crown. The bold statement of their hopes for the Church – the *Confession of Faith* – by the Reformation parliament was, however, both rather ambitious and of dubious legality. The Church had no official policy, structure or financial settlement, and although the *First Book of Discipline* – a 'mission statement', declaring their aims for the new church, including organisation, education and practice – was drafted and accepted, lack of trained ministers meant that a well-organised national church would not evolve until almost a century later.

No account of these events would be complete without mentioning John Knox. Ordained as a priest, he was much influenced by George Wishart, and joined Cardinal Beaton's murderers at St Andrews Castle during the siege there. He was taken prisoner by the French, but between 1549 and 1553 established a reputation in England for preaching radical Protestant ideas. During his time in Geneva, he was influenced by the ideas of John Calvin, and in 1555 made a preaching tour in Scotland, where he found support from many lords and landowners. He returned to Scotland during the final years of Mary of Guise's Regency, and was involved in the drafting of the *First Book of Discipline*.

Although the motives for rejecting the Roman form of worship may have been spiritual, for some political and economic reasons were equally important. It was true that later Stewart monarchs – James IV and James V – had perhaps abused the royal prerogative that had been granted to James III. This allowed the Crown to make their own appointments, and as a result several natural sons of the Stewart kings had been promoted to lucrative positions in the Church. However, the monarchs were not alone in benefiting from this system as quite a few other families of the Scottish nobility also 'acquired' the revenue of ecclesiastical properties by appointing commendators from their own families. Commendators were originally clerics who carried out the administrative work of the benefices, but by the 16th century some were laymen. After the Reformation, former Church lands were parcelled out to the nobility.

Equally relevant to the progress of the Reformation were the political relations between Protestant England, Catholic France, and Scotland. It was ultimately English intervention on the side of the Protestant party which helped to bring about the 1560 declaration; but it was also the Francophile policies of Mary of Guise which had alienated some of the Scottish nobles.

The *Confession of Faith* abolished the Latin mass and papal supremacy; rejected transubstantiation; reduced the number of sacraments to two; and stressed the importance of the vernacular in preaching, education and instruction. Also there was to be increased participation by the laity, in worship, administration and congregational discipline. To this 'democratic' end, a hierarchy of church committees was formed – kirk, presbytery, synod and General Assembly – where there would be clerical and lay representation. Although this organisation was formed in theory, it took many years before presbyteries were properly up and running.

There were just as many problems with the training of Reformed ministers; supervision of the different areas; and the financial settlement of the Church. The Church continued to rely heavily on the Crown for financial support, and for the rest of the century and into the next there was a long debate about their relationship. This would eventually result in the re-introduction of bishops by Charles I, leading to further bloodshed over religion, but during the heady days of post-1560 Scotland certain aspects of the new Church were greeted enthusiastically.

The removal of idolatrous monuments and religious images, as well as the abolishment of veneration of relics, meant that the majority of pre-Reformation churches continued to be used after being cleared. Some churches, however, were built to a new design – notably Burntisland Parish Church, which was build in 1595; and Greyfriars in Edinburgh. Burntisland was one of the first post-Reformation churches in Scotland, built to a solid square plan. The act of worship was to be a congregate act with no barrier between the minister and congregation: no rood screen; no nave and no chancel.

The removal of idolatrous images from the Church, including statues, also meant that the polyphonic singing of church choirs – which had been a major feature of the abbeys and monasteries – was abandoned. The beautiful music of the Scottish composer Robert Carver; the few carvings that survive – even carved

Burntisland Parish Church – built following the Reformation

crosses were seen as idolatrous – and the illuminated mistrals and books of hours which do remain, would have been lost to posterity if the Reformers had been entirely successful in their destruction. As it was, both Church and State co-operated to attempt to remove all popular vestiges of pre-Reformation worship, such as feasts and festivals.

Human habit – or need – to continue certain traditions, however, conspired deliberately, or otherwise, to frustrate their attempts. Thus, throughout the 17th century, church records tell of visits to healing wells for cures; and the perpetuation of rites which were regarded as papistical. Although festivals and feasts may have had religious origins, they developed secular purposes for markets and other legal purposes, which were equally important in day-to-day life. The practice of allowing funerary effigies to be placed inside the church building was also halted, although several fine examples of pre- and post-Reformation tombs remain today.

UNREST AND UPHEAVAL – COVENANT TO DISRUPTION

During the remainder of the 16th century and into the 17th, the religious settlement in Scotland continued to cause problems, particularly during the reigns of James VI and Charles I. In the early part of the 17th century, James's ecclesiastical policies re-introduced certain features of Episcopacy – the administration of the Church by bishops – which were as much a result of his own religious convictions as lack of unity within the Church.

At the time of the Reformation, the Church had relied on the support of the nobles to achieve religious and political goals, but during the 1580s to 1630s there was much criticism of some of the nobles, who were seen to be not fulfilling their role as godly magistrates. One of the main critics, and especially critical of God's chief magistrate – the King himself – was Andrew Melville, regarded by many as being the real force behind the introduction of the Presbyterian system. He argued vehemently against any lay interference in Church organisation.

During this period, the lack of co-operation or communication between Church and State led to stalemate. Despite the Church's rejection of the Crown's involvement in Church policy, James issued, and was able to get the General Assembly to ratify, certain acts which gradually reduced the power of the Reformers.

The *Black Act* of 1584 removed the authority of the 13 presbyteries over Church matters, although the *Golden Act* of 1592 did restore this power. But the *Five Articles of Perth* of 1618, which had initially been rejected at the General Assembly at St Andrews the previous year, re-introduced kneeling at prayer, private communion, confirmation by bishop, observance of holy days and private baptism;

all of which, although an illustration of James's belief in his divine right authority, actually contributed to the eventual protest and strife of the 1630s and later.

Charles I continued his father's autocratic attitude to the Church, but this only provoked unity among his opponents. Charles's introduction of the *Common Prayer Book* in 1637 resulted in the signing of the *National Covenant* in 1638, asserting the people's right to have a Reformed Church, administered without interference from the King. The Covenant was first signed by a small group of nobles in February 1638 at Greyfriars Kirkyard, in Edinburgh, and at the General Assembly of that year, Charles's prayer book was banned, along with the *Five Articles of Perth*. Charles attempted to restore his authority with the Bishops War of 1639 and 1640, but the outcome was mixed and a short uneasy peace followed.

Initially the Covenanters were successful, and Charles acquiesced to their demands in order to calm the situation in England and Ireland. In 1643 the *Solemn League and Covenant* – a religious and military pact between the Parliamentarians, in England, and the Covenanters, in Scotland – was signed, but was never fully accepted by the English. Charles, however, was defeated by a combined English and Scottish army at Marston Moor in 1644.

In Scotland the Marquis of Montrose led a rising for the King and defeated Covenanting armies at Tippermuir, Aberdeen, Inverlochy, Alford and Kilsyth. However, the Covenanting General, David Leslie eventually defeated Montrose at Philiphaugh in 1645. Charles surrendered to the Scots' army at Newark, but

Greyfriars, Edinburgh – the National Covenant was signed here in 1638

Churches and Abbeys of Scotland

this did little to resolve the crisis. Charles was executed in 1649. The Scots rose against Cromwell, but were defeated at Dunbar in 1650, and the Cromwellian administration of Scotland attempted to reduce the power of the Covenanters.

With the restoration of Charles II in 1660 came the reintroduction of bishops in 1662. Even before this, in 1660, an act was passed banning conventicles – Covenanters meeting to worship as they pleased – as a result of fear of religious opposition. In 1666 the Covenanters rose and marched on Edinburgh, but their ill-armed troop was routed at Rullion Green in the Pentland Hills. Peace was still not achieved, and in 1679 the Covenanters rebelled again after the murder of Archbishop James Sharp. Despite an early success at Drumclog, they were defeated in 1679 at Bothwell Brig.

The most extreme group of the Covenanters, the Cameronians – who denounced the King's authority – led by James Cameron, continued the struggle until 1680, when they were surprised at Airds Moss and Cameron was slain. During the 1680s, the Covenanters were persecuted, many being executed by government forces, during the period now known as the *Killing Times*. The Highlands also suffered severely.

John Graham of Claverhouse, *Bonnie Dundee* or *Bloody Clavers,* was responsible for many of the killings, including two of the most famous, the 'Wigtown Martyrs', in 1685. Margaret Lauchleson or McLachlan and Margaret Wilson were sentenced to death because of their Cameronian beliefs. Although they were tethered to posts to be drowned by the incoming tide, they may have been rescued. There is a monument to the two women in Wigtown graveyard.

Charles II died in 1685, and his brother, James VII – a Catholic – came to the throne. The Revolution of 1689, which replaced James with the Protestant William of Orange and Mary, confirmed the Westminster confession, and a Presbyterian form of Church government, but there remained small groups of dissenters. Families and individuals remained loyal to the openly Catholic Stewarts or the Catholic religion itself. Much of this support withered, however, when the Stewarts were decisively defeated at the Battle of Culloden in 1746.

A series of secessions within the church took place during the 18th and 19th centuries, the first in 1733. These were again mainly over the relationship between Church and State: who had control over appointments of ministers. The General Assembly had decided that only elders and heritors would elect ministers, excluding the congregation. As this denied the 'democratic' principles of the Presbyterian Church, a group, led by Ebenezer Erskine, broke away, arguing for the disestablishment of the Church. Later seceders divided off – and up – over other issues, but the common feature was patronage. The Burghers, Anti-Burghers, Auld Lights, New Lights, and the Relief Church were all established as alternatives to the Church of Scotland.

The *Disruption* of 1843 was also about patronage. The *Ten Year Conflict* started in 1833 between the Evangelicals and the Moderates. The Evangelicals had passed the Chapel and Veto acts, which allowed congregations to veto unsuitable ministers appointed by the patrons or heritors. The legality of these acts was put to the test at Auchterarder, where the candidate Robert Young was rejected by the congregation. In 1843 the *Chapel Act* was vetoed, and the following year Thomas Chalmers, leader of the Evangelicals, dramatically left the General Assembly, followed by 474 other ministers and set up the Free Church.

The Free Church took about 40% of the membership of the Church of Scotland with it, and in its first few years attracted much popularity and money to help build new churches. By the 1860s, however, the majority of the congregations were middle-class, much like the established Church. In the Highlands the Free Church remained – and remains – popular, as it supported the crofters during their disputes with landowners in the 1880s.

Catholicism re-emerged as a major force in Scotland, as large numbers of Irish immigrants settled from the 1850s. The Scottish Episcopal Church; Judaism; Temperance movements; Muslims; Sikhs; Buddhists; New-Age Celtic Christians all have established themselves, to greater or lesser degree, during the 20th and 21st century.

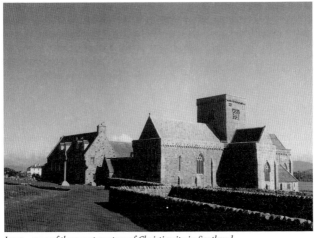

Iona – one of the great centres of Christianity in Scotland

Map of Sites (Locations may be approximate)

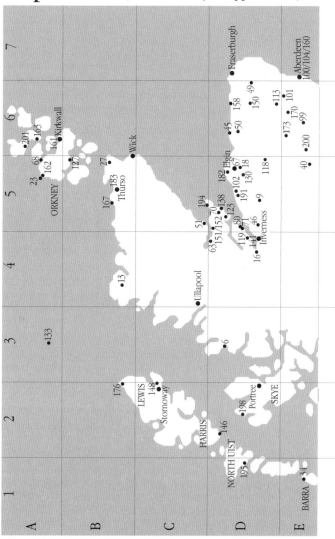

Churches and Abbeys of Scotland

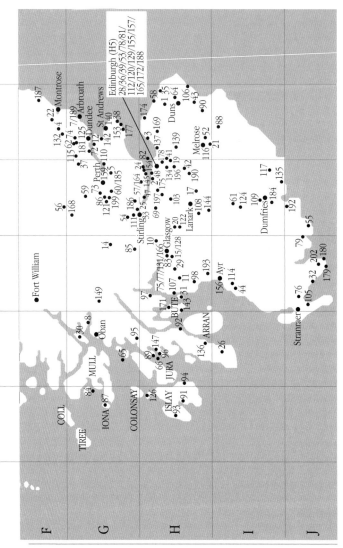

Edinburgh (H5)
28/36/39/53/78/81/
112/120/129/155/157/
165/172/188

●187

●132/4
Montrose
●22
●7/189
Arbroath
115 627
181 125
Dundee
St Andrews
140
138
153
177

58 1 35
174 64
Duns 106
●90
●43
88
169
58
139
Melrose
116 52
21

86 73 Perth
110
142
3
137
78
41
196 19 42
134 175
190
144
108
Lanark 17
122
20 Glasgow
103
69 197
2 48
57/164 24
159
37
59
168
56
12
●199 60/185
54
111
Stirling 33 5
10

14
85

77/131 166
75/7
83 107
29 15/128
11
143 31
BUTE
92
71
97
149

30
8
Oban
95

65
89 147 96
66
JURA 94
136

126
COLONSAY
93 91
ISLAY

COLL

TIREE

IONA●87
84
MULL

Fort William●

98
156 Ayr
114
44
193
26
ARRAN

61
124
109 184 135
Dumfries 192
79
55
202 180
76 179
105 32
Stranraer

F
G
H
I
J

Churches, Abbeys and Other Sacred Sites

Abbey St Bathans

[1 (H6)] Off A6112/B6355, 5.5 miles N of Duns, Borders. (NGR: NT 758623 LR: 67)

This is the site of a Cistercian nunnery, founded in the 12th century by Ada Countess of Dunbar and dedicated to St Mary the Virgin, but burned by the English in 1543-4. The church continued to be used, but has been reduced in length and only parts of the east and north wall are original. There is a worn stone effigy of a prioress. Nearby is a spring [NT 761620] which was believed to have healing powers, and was dedicated to St Bathan. It is said that the water never freezes, no matter how cold the weather.

Abercorn Church and Museum

[2 (H5)] Off A904, 5 miles E of Linlithgow, Hopetoun Estate. (NGR: NT 083792 LR: 65)

One of the first bishoprics in Scotland was founded here in 670 as part of the Anglian church of Northumbria, which included Hexham, York and Lindisfarne. It was abandoned after the Battle of Nechtansmere in 685. The present church, dedicated to St Serf (the original dedication was to St Wilfred), mostly dates from the Reformation until the present day, although part may be from the 11th century, and it is built on an older site mentioned by the Venerable Bede. There are two Norse hogback burial stones, a wheel cross-stone decorated with a flower, and a cross-shaft dating from the 7th century, as well as burial aisles, the Hopetoun Gallery and Dalyell aisle, and an interesting burial ground.

Explanatory displays. Disabled access. Car Parking.

Open all year, daily.

Tel: 01506 834331 (Nimmo, Session clerk)

Aberlady Parish Church

[3 (H6)] Off A198, 3.5 miles NW of Haddington, Main Street, Aberlady, East Lothian. (NGR: NT 462798 LR: 66)

The body of the church was remodelled in 1886, but the strong tower dates from the 15th century and the building incorporates burial aisles from the 16th and 17th centuries. The church may have been dedicated to St Mary, and houses a cross-shaft, stained glass, and a marble monument attributed to Canova.

Sales area. Disabled access. Parking nearby.

Open May-Sep, 8.00-dusk.

Tel: 01875 853137/870237

Aberlemno Carved Stones (HS)

[4 (F6)] Off B9134, 6 miles NE of Forfar, Angus. (NGR: NO 523557 LR: 54)

A magnificent group of Pictish carved stones, the most impressive and elaborate of which is the cross-slab in

Aberlemno churchyard. One side has a full-length cross, decorated with intricate inter-laced designs and surrounded by intertwining animals. The other side is framed by two ser-pents, which surround a depic-tion of a battle, believed to be the Battle of Nechtansmere in 685 when the Picts routed a Northumbrian army.

The church dates from 1722, but stands on a much older site: a church is said to have been founded here by Nechtan, King of Picts, around the turn of the 8th century, although it is not mentioned until the 13th cen-tury. It was probably dedicated to St Peter by St Curitan, and houses an ancient octagonal-carved font.

A second cross-slab stands by the roadside in Aberlemno, with a full-length cross and angels and beasts on one side, and Pictish symbols and other carvings on the other. Also by the roadside are two other stones, one a Pictish carved stone, the other an unadorned standing stone.

Parking nearby but may be problematic for the three stones by B9134.

Accessible all year – stones enclosed for protection from Oct-Apr and cannot be viewed during this time.

Abernethy Round Tower (HS)

[5 (G5)] On A913, 6 miles SE of Perth, Abernethy, Perthshire. (NGR: NO 190165 LR: 58)

A monastery, dedicated to St Bride, is said to have been founded here by nuns from Kildare around 625, but nothing remains of a once important centre except the imposing 74-foot round tower, which dates from the 11th century and a later

Culdee establishment. There are only two Irish-style towers remaining in mainland Scotland (the other is at Brechin Cathedral), and there are good views from the top. A fine Pictish carved stone is located at the base of the tower, and there are also the remains of jougs.

There was an Augustinian priory here in 1272, later replaced by a collegiate church, but there are no remains.

There is also an interesting museum at School Wynd.

Parking Nearby

Open Apr-Sep – for access apply to key holder.

Tel: 0131 668 8800 (tower)/ 01738 850889 (museum)

Applecross

[6 (D3)] Off A896, Applecross, 1 mile N of village, Ross-shire. (NGR: NG 713458 LR: 24)

This is the site of a monastery, founded by St Maelrubha in 673, and said to have been destroyed by Norsemen. Applecross became a place of pilgrimage, and earth taken from Maelrubha's grave was said to ensure a safe return. An 8th-century cross-slab stands by the gate of the church, and is said to mark the grave of Ruairidh Mor MacAogan, an abbot of Applecross, who died around 800. Inside the modern church (which is open daily) there are a further three fragments, found at the east end of the burial ground. While the existing church dates from 1817, the nearby ruinous chapel (roofed over by bushes growing up inside the walls) was built in the 15th century. There is a spring [NG 717450], with steps down to it near the road west of Applecross House. It is said to be a holy well, and was dedicated to Maelrubha.

Parking nearby.

Access at all reasonable times.

Arbroath Abbey (HS)

[7 (G6)] Off A92, Arbroath, Angus. (NGR: NO 643413 LR: 54)

Impressive parts of the cruciform church survive, including the fine west end, south transept and sacristy, as well as the gatehouse and Abbot's House, which houses a museum. The cloister and other domestic buildings are very ruinous, but their foundations are laid out in the grass. There is a large burial ground.

The abbey was founded as a Tironensian establishment in 1178 by William the Lion, in memory of his friend Thomas a Becket (St Thomas the Martyr). William was buried here in 1214, and the Monymusk Reliquary was also kept at the abbey. The Declaration of Arbroath was signed here in 1320, asserting Scottish independence over English aggression, and Mary, Queen of Scots visited in 1562. The Stone of Destiny was placed before the high altar after being taken from Westminster Abbey in 1951 – the Stone is now at Edinburgh Castle. There is a museum in Arbroath, and some distance away is the old parish church of Arbroath and carved stones museum, both at St Vigeans (see separate entry).

Explanatory displays in visitor centre and Abbot's House. Audio-visual presentations. Gift shop. WC. Explanatory boards. Parking nearby. £.

Open all year: Apr-Sep, daily 9.30-18.30; Oct-Mar, Mon-Sat 9.00-16.30, Sun 14.00-16.30; closed 25/26 Dec & 1/2 Jan.

Tel: 01241 878756

Ardchattan Priory (HS)

[8 (G3)] Off A828, 6.5 miles NE of Oban, Argyll. (NGR: NM 971349 LR: 49)

Set in a peaceful location, Ardchattan Priory, a Valliscaulian establishment dedicated to St Mary and John the Baptist, or St Modan (although the name Ardchattan suggests an association with St Catan), was founded in 1231 by Duncan Mac-Dougall. Robert the Bruce held a parliament here in 1309. Colin Campbell of Glenure, murdered in 1752, is buried here – his death features in the novel *Kidnapped* by Robert Louis Stevenson.

The atmospheric ruins consist of part of the priory church, which was used by the parish until 1731. This is in the care of Historic Scotland, and houses 16th-century carved grave slabs, a finely carved stone sarcophagus, and an early Christian carved wheel cross. Other buildings were incorporated into a mansion, and there is a four-acre garden.

Facilities as gardens. Guidebook. Tea room (open May-Aug, Sun-Fri 11.00-17.00, closed Sat). WC. Disabled access. Car and limited coach parking. £ (gardens)/ priory ruins free.

Ruins of priory (Historic Scotland) open all reasonable times; house NOT open; gardens (privately owned) open Apr-Oct, daily 9.00-18.00.

Tel: 0131 668 8800 (HS)/01631 750274   Fax: 0131 668 8888 (HS)/01631 750238

Ardclach Bell Tower (HS)

[9 (D5)] Off A939, 8.5 miles SE of Nairn. (NGR: NH 953453 LR: 27)

The detached bell tower, built in 1655 and two-storeys high, stands on a hill above the parish church. It was used to summon worshippers to church, as well as a prison and watchtower: the lower storey is windowless while the upper has small windows and shot-holes.

Access at all reasonable times – apply to key holder.

Tel: 01667 460232

Auld Kirk Museum, Kirkintilloch

[10 (H4)] Off A803, 6.5 miles NE of Glasgow, The Cross, Kirkintilloch.
(NGR: NS 655743 LR: 64)

The old parish church of St Mary's, dating from 1644 and cruciform in plan with corbiestepped gables, now houses a museum with displays on the Romans, local industry and home life. The church has large pointed windows.

Explanatory displays. Gift shop. Disabled access. Car parking.

Open all year, Tue-Sat 10.00-13.00 and 14.00-17.00; closed Sun and Mon.

Tel: 0141 578 0144   Fax: 0141 578 0140

Auld Kirk of Kilbirnie

[11 (H4)] Off B780, 7.5 miles E of Largs, Dalry Road, Kilbirnie, Ayrshire.
(NGR: NS 314546 LR: 63)

St Brendan founded a monastery here in the 6th-century (hence the name Kilbirnie), but there are no remains. The nave of the present church dates from 1470, and the small tower from 1490. An aisle was added in 1597 for the Cunninghams of Glengarnock, and there is fine Italian Renaissance-style carving, dating from 1642, in the Crawfurd aisle. There are interesting markers in the kirkyard.

Sales area. WC. Disabled access. Parking nearby.

Open Jul-Aug, Tue-Fri 14.00-16.00; other times by appt.

Tel: 01505 683459

Balmerino Abbey (NTS)

[12 (G6)] Off A914, 4.5 miles SW of Newport on Tay, Balmerino, Fife.
(NGR: NO 358246 LR: 59)

The scant but picturesque ruins of the abbey stand in a peaceful setting near the south shore of the Firth of Tay. It was a Cistercian establishment, founded by Ermengarde (who was buried here), widow of William the Lion, and their son, Alexander II, in 1229. The abbey was dedicated to St Mary and St Edward.

  It was torched by the English in 1547 and ransacked by a Reforming mob in 1559, and only the basement of the chapter house and adjoining buildings survive, while only foundations remain of the church. Mary, Queen of Scots, stayed

for two days at the abbey in 1565. There is an old Spanish chestnut tree, said to have been planted by the monks.
Parking nearby.

Access at all reasonable times.

Tel: 0131 243 9300
Fax: 0131 243 9301

Balnakeil Church

[13 (B4)] Off A838, 0.5 miles NW of Durness, Balnakeil, Sutherland, Highland.
(NGR: NC 391687 LR: 9)

The site here was dedicated to St Maelrubha, but the ruins of the present T-plan church date substantially from the 17th century. There are some interesting markers

in the burial ground, including to Robert Calder Mackay (Rob Donn) the 'Burns of the North', who died in 1778.
Parking.

Access at all reasonable times.

Balquhidder Kirk

[14 (G4)] Off A84, 14 miles NW of Callendar, Balquhidder, Stirlingshire.
(NGR: NN 535209 LR: 57)

Balquhidder is associated with St Angus. St Angus's Stone (Clach Aenais), dates from as early as the 8th century, and was said to have marked his burial (it has been moved to the north wall of the later church). It was 'removed [from the old church] to destroy a superstitious desire that existed among the parishioners to stand or kneel on it during a marriage or baptism'. There are fine carved slabs in the burial ground, including ones for Rob Roy MacGregor (who died in 1734), his wife, and two of his sons. The old church, which is dated 1631, is very ruinous, while the modern Gothic-style church dates from 1853 and was designed by David Bryce. The later church, which is open daily, has a 17th-century bell, old Gaelic bibles, and an exhibition on the history of the church.
Parking nearby.

Access at all reasonable times.

Barochan Cross (HS)

[15 (H4)] Off A737, Paisley Abbey, Paisley, Renfrewshire. (NGR: NS 486640 LR: 64)

A fine free-standing carved cross, large but weathered, sculpted with warriors and human figures, which dates from as early as the 8th century. It formerly stood at Mill of Barochan, in Houston parish west of Paisley, but is now housed in Paisley Abbey: also see separate entry.

Explanatory displays. Gift shop. Tearoom. WC. Parking Nearby.

Paisley Abbey: open all year, Mon-Sat 10.00-15.30, Sun services only.

Tel: 0141 889 7654

Beauly Priory (HS)

[16 (D4)] On A862, 10 miles W of Inverness, Highland. (NGR: NH 527465 LR: 26)

The fine ruined cruciform church survives of a Valliscaulian priory, dedicated to St Mary and St John the Baptist, and founded in 1230 by John Bisset and Alexander II. The priory was plundered in 1506, became a Cistercian house around 1510, and Mary, Queen of Scots, visited in 1564. The church was roofless by 1633, and the cloister and domestic buildings were demolished, much of the stone being used by Cromwell to built a fort at Inverness in 1650. The north transept was restored in 1901 as it was used as the Mackenzies of Kintail burial aisle. There are fine windows, and several old burial slabs and tombs, one for a Prior Mackenzie. There is a museum in Beauly.

Parking.

Access at reasonable times.

Biggar Kirk

[17 (H5)] Off A72 or A702, Manse, High Street, Biggar. (NGR: NT 042378 LR: 72)

The impressive cruciform church, with a crenellated tower pierced by gunloops, was made into a collegiate establishment, dedicated to St Mary, by Malcolm Lord Fleming in 1545. It probably incorporates older work, as it was established in the original parish church of St Nicholas. It was restored in the 1870s and again in

the 1930s, is still used as a parish church, and there are good examples of modern stained glass. The burial ground has markers to the Gladstone family.
Explanatory displays. Sales area. Induction loop for church services. Car parking.
Open during summer months, daily 9.00-1700; other times key from Moat Park Heritage Centre, which is opposite the kirk.
Tel: 01899 211050

Birnie Kirk

[18 (D5)] Off B9010, 2.5 miles S of Elgin, Moray. (NGR: NJ 206587 LR: 28)
There was a Culdee establishment here, and a weathered Pictish carved stone, decorated with an eagle, is located in the oval burial ground. The fine church stands on a mound, and the chancel arch, the north and south doorways, and the font date from the early 12th century. The church is dedicated to St Brendan, has an ancient bell (the Ronnel Bell), and was altered in 1734 and 1891. It was here that the Bishops of Moray had a cathedral before moving to Elgin.
Parking.
Stone: access at all reasonable times.
Tel: 01343 542621

Borthwick Parish Church

[19 (H5)] Off A7, 2 miles SE of Gorebridge, Midlothian. (NGR: NT 369597 LR: 66)
The Gothic church, with a tall spire, mostly dates from the 19th century after its 11th-century predecessor was burnt out in 1775. Parts of the old church were retained, including the apse, south transept and the Dundas of Arniston burial vault. The original church was dedicated to St Mungo, and there are two fine, detailed 15th-century stone effigies of William Borthwick and his wife. Borthwick built the magnificent Borthwick Castle (which is now a hotel).
WC. Disabled access. Induction loop for church services. Car and coach parking.
Open all year, daily.

Bothwell Parish Church

[20 (H5)] Off A725, 2 miles N of Hamilton, Main Street, Bothwell. (NGR: NS 705586 LR: 64)
Archibald the Grim, Earl of Douglas, founded a collegiate establishment in 1398, dedicated to St Bride, although there was a church here from the 6th century. The church has a medieval chancel, although the tall tower and nave date from 1833, and the building was altered and reunited in 1933. There are 17th- and 18th-century monuments, including to the Earls of Douglas and Duke of Hamilton, as well as fine stained glass. There is an interesting burial ground.
Guides tours available 10.30-16.00. Sales area. WC. Disabled access. Parking nearby.
Open Easter-Sep, daily.
Tel: 01698 853189 Fax: 01698 853229 Email: bothwell@presbyteryofhamilton.co.uk

Bowden Kirk

[21 (H6)] Off A699, 5 miles E of Selkirk, Bowden, Borders. (NGR: NT 554303 LR: 73)

The long rectangular church incorporates work from the 15th and 17th centuries, and is known to have been established by 1128 and dedicated to St Bathan. The building was remodelled in 1794 and again in 1909, but has a carved 17th-century laird's loft of the Kerrs. There are the burial vaults for the Dukes of Roxburghe and Riddell-Carre family, as well as a memorial to Lady Grizel Baillie. There are interesting markers in the burial ground, and the church stands on the pilgrim route, St Cuthbert's Way, from Melrose to Lindisfarne.

WC. Disabled access. Parking nearby.

Open all year during daylight hours.

Brechin Cathedral

[22 (F6)] Off A90, Brechin, Angus. (NGR: NO 596601 LR: 44)

There was a Culdee establishment here, and next to the imposing cathedral is an unusual 11th-century round tower, believed to have been used to store precious relics. Only two of these towers survive in Scotland, the other being at Abernethy (see separate entry). The cathedral, dedicated to the Holy Trinity and dating from the 13th century, has a tower and spire at one end. It was sympathetically restored in 1900-02, has an aisled nave and rebuilt choir, and is used as the parish church. There is a fine Pictish cross-slab, and other fragments, including the 9th-century St Mary's Stone and an ancient octagonal-shaped font, as well as

excellent modern stained glass. There are some interesting markers in the burial ground. Brechin Museum has collections relating to the cathedral.

Parking nearby. Sales area.

Open all year, daily 9.00-17.00.

Tel: 01356 629360

Brough of Birsay (HS)

[23 (A5)] Off A966, 13 miles N of Stromness, Birsay, Orkney. (NGR: HY 239285 LR: 6)

An early Christian monastery was established here on the tidal island. This was later used by Norsemen, and Earl Thorfinn had a house here. There was a substantial 12th-century church, consisting of a rectangular nave, smaller chancel and an apse. There are also the foundations of an enclosure wall, as well as several other buildings. A fine Pictish carved stone was found here, the original is now in the Museum of Scotland, while a replica is on the islet. The island is reached by a causeway, which floods at high tide.

Parking nearby. £. Combined ticket available for all Orkney monuments.

Open mid Jun-Sep, daily 9.00-18.30, last ticket 18.00.

Tel: 01856 721205

Burntisland Parish Church

[24 (H5)] Off A921, 4 miles SW of Kirkcaldy, East Leven Street, Burntisland, Fife. (NGR: NT 234857 LR: 66)

This is one of the first post-Reformation churches built in Scotland, dating from 1592-4, and has an unusual square design with a central tower and octagonal belfry. The mariners' loft has painted panels, and the church is still in use. The General Assembly met here in 1601, in the presence of James VI, when a new translation of the Bible was approved.

Sales area. WC. Parking nearby. Church tours arranged by curator: also for visits to Burntisland Heritage Centre.

Open Jun-Aug, daily 10.00-12.00 and 14.00-16.00; other times key available from church officer or curator.

Tel: 01592 873275 curator/01592 872011 church officer

Cambuskenneth Abbey (HS)

[25 (G5)] Off A907, 1 mile E of Stirling, Cambuskenneth. (NGR: NS 809939 LR: 57)

The abbey, at one time a rich establishment, was founded in 1147 by David I, was later a house of Augustinian canons, and dedicated to the Blessed Virgin Mary. It was here that in 1304 Robert the Bruce and Bishop Lamberton signed a bond of mutual assistance, and Bruce held a parliament at the abbey in 1326, when the nobles swore allegiance to his heir, later David II. James III was buried here after being murdered at Sauchieburn in 1488, as is Margaret of Denmark, his queen.

The abbey was ransacked in 1559, and the impressive detached bell-tower is the only substantial part remaining, although remains survive of other parts, including the fine west door. Materials were taken from the building to construct Mar's Wark in Stirling.

Parking nearby.

Open Apr-Sep, daily 9.00-18.30 – view exterior only: keys available locally.

Campbeltown Cross

[26 (13)] Off A83, NE of Main Street, Campbeltown, Kintyre.
(NGR: NR 720204 LR: 68)

A finely carved 15th-century cross, decorated on one side with interweave, while the other side has figures of saints, including St Michael slaying the dragon. The cross was brought here from Kilkivan, near Machrihanish, in the 17th century to be used as the market cross of Campbeltown. It shares many features with the cross at Kilchoman (see separate entry) on Islay.

Parking nearby.

Access at all reasonable times.

Canisbay Parish Church

[27 (B5)] On A836, 15 miles N of Wick, Kirkstyle, Caithness, Highland.
(NGR: ND 343729 LR: 12)

Overlooking the Pentland Firth, the long white-washed church, which dates from the 15th century and later, is mentioned in the 13th century and was dedicated to St Drostan. It is built on a mound covering the remains of a broch, and is cruciform in shape with a small tower at one end. There is a memorial to the de Groot or Groat family, best known from nearby John o' Groats, and many interesting markers in the burial ground. It is recorded that, as late as 1700, local people would go round the church on their knees, and then wash in water from the burn. This did not please the Presbyterian minister of the time.

Access at all reasonable times.

Canongate Kirk, Edinburgh

[28 (H5)] Canongate (Royal Mile), opposite Huntly House. (NGR: NT 262738 LR: 66)
The striking church, cruciform in plan with aisles, was begun in 1688, and has been well restored. It is the parish church of Holyroodhouse and Edinburgh Castle, and there is an interesting burial ground with fine memorials: David Rizzio is buried here, as is Adam Smith; the publishers James and John Ballantyne; the poet Robert Ferguson; and Agnes McLehose, who was Robert Burns's Clarinda.
Guided tours by appt. Information available in many languages. Refreshments. Disabled access. Parking nearby.
Church: open Jun-Sep, Mon-Sat 10.30-16.30; burial ground open all year.
Tel: 0131 556 3515   Fax: 0131 557 5847

Castle Semple Collegiate Church (HS)

[29 (H4)] Off B7776, 7 miles SW of Paisley, Castle Semple. (NGR: NS 377601 LR: 63)
The long rectangular church, dedicated to St Mary, with a tower at one end, has a three-sided apse pierced by unusual windows. It is ruinous but stands to the wallhead, and houses the elaborate tomb of John, 1st Lord Semple, who established the church in 1504 and was killed at the Battle of Flodden in 1513.
Parking nearby.
Access at all reasonable times.

Cathedral of St Moluag and Parish Church

[30 (G3)] Off B8045, 1.5 miles N of Achnacroish, Lismore. (NGR: NM 860434 LR: 49)
The church, once used as the Cathedral of Argyll and the Isles after the bishopric was transferred here in 1236, is a fine building although much reduced in size (it was 125 feet long at one time). The 14th-century choir of the church was restored in 1749 with the lowering of the walls by as much as 10 feet, but only foundations remain of the nave and tower. There is a traditional baptismal font, as well as an exhibition on 800 years of Christianity on Lismore. Several carved slabs, dating from medieval times, are in the burial ground.
Parking nearby. Donations welcome.
Access at all reasonable times.

Cathedral of the Isles, Millport

[31 (H4)] Off A860, College Street, Millport, Great Cumbrae. (NGR: NS 166553 LR: 63)
Britain's smallest cathedral, dating from 1851 and designed by William Butterfield. The cathedral, dedicated to the Holy Spirit, has fine stained glass, and there is a collection of carved stones from Mid Kirkton.
Parking. Sales area. Picnic area. WC. Retreat House: accommodation available.
Open all year, daily.
Tel: 01475 530353   Fax: 01475 530204   Email: tccumbrae@argyll.anglican.org

Chapel Finian (HS)

[32 (J4)] On A747, 11 miles SE of Glenluce, Mochrum, Dumfries and Galloway.
(NGR: NX 278489   LR: 82)

Foundations survive of a small rectangular chapel, dating from the 10th or 11th century, standing in a 50-foot-wide enclosure. The chapel was dedicated to St Finian of Moville.

Parking nearby.

Access at all reasonable times.

Church of the Holy Rude, Stirling

[33 (H5)] Off A9, St John Street (near Stirling Castle), Stirling. (NGR: NS 793937   LR: 57)

The splendid aisled church, cruciform in plan, was built in the 16th and 17th centuries and dedicated to the Holy Rude (the cross on which Jesus was crucified). There is an imposing tower at the west end, and part of the church has an original medieval timber roof. The church was used for the Coronation of James VI in 1567, at which John Knox preached (other Scottish Kings and Queen worshipped here, including Mary, Queen of Scots) and is still used as a parish church. There is a magnificent pipe organ and fine stained glass windows. The historic churchyard has many interesting memorials and

spectacular views of Stirling Castle and area. Stirling Castle, Cowane's Hospital, Mar's Wark and Argyll's Lodging are nearby.

Sales area. WC. Disabled access. Car parking.

Open May-Sep, Mon-Sat 10.00-17.00.

Tel: 01786 471848   Fax: 01786 471088   Email: tfgmacdoug@aol.com

---

Cille Bharra

[34 (E1)] Off A888, 6 miles N of Castlebay, Eoligarry, N end of Barra.
(NGR: NF 704077 LR: 31)

St Barr or Finnbar of Cork established a church here in the 7th century, but the ruinous medieval church dates from the 12th century. Two chapels also survive, one of which has been reroofed to provide shelter for several carved slabs from the churchyard, some of which may have been used to mark the burials of the MacNeils of Barra and their kin. Mass is said here on the feasts of the Celtic saints. Other interesting slabs lie in the yard, while a fine carved stone of the 10th or 11th century – with a cross and runic inscription – is kept in the Museum of Scotland: a cast is displayed at Cille Bharra. The inscription reads: 'after Thorgerth, Steiner's daughter, this cross was raised'.

Parking nearby.
Access at all reasonable times.

Coldingham Priory Church

[35 (H6)] Off A1107, 2.5 miles NW of Eyemouth, Coldingham, Berwickshire, Borders.
(NGR: NT 904659 LR: 67)

St Ebba (Abb) is said to have established a monastery at St Abb's Head in the 7th century, but this was destroyed by Norsemen. The priory was refounded, possibly in the 12th century, at Coldingham, and was dedicated to St Mary, St Ebba and St Cuthbert. It was sacked in 1216, 1419 and 1544 by the English. Mary, Queen of Scots, stayed here in 1566, but most of the priory was destroyed by Cromwell's forces in 1648. The choir of the priory was used as the parish church, part was rebuilt in the 17th century, and it was renovated in the 1850s and 1954. There is a detailed model of the priory in the church, and modern stained glass windows. Some fragments of the other priory buildings survive, including an arch from the original church.

Open May-Sep, Wed 14.00-16.00 or by appt.
Tel: 01890 771280

Corstorphine Old Parish Church

[36 (H5)] Kirk Loan, Corstorphine, Edinburgh. (NGR: NT 201728 LR: 66)

A collegiate church, dedicated to St John the Baptist, was established here in 1429 by the older parish church of St Mary, although it is the older building that has gone. The present building has a stone-slabbed roof and a 15th-century squat tower with a short spire. There are heraldic panels and the tombs of Sir Adam Forrester, Lord Provost of Edinburgh who died in 1405; and Sir John Forrester, Lord Chamberlain during the reign of James I. There are modern stained glass windows and an interesting burial ground. Nothing survives of a once important castle of the Forresters, which stood near here, except for a large doocot (off Saughton Road North). There is also a fine sycamore tree.

Sales area. Limited disabled access. Parking nearby.

Open Feb-Nov, Wed 10.30-12.00.

Coupar Angus Abbey

[37 (G5)] On A923, 12 miles NE of Perth, just S of Coupar Angus, Perthshire.
(NGR: NO 223397 LR: 53)

Little remains of what was a rich abbey, except a ruined gatehouse and some fragments. It was founded in 1164 by Malcolm IV, and was a Cistercian establishment, dedicated to the Blessed Virgin Mary. The buildings were burned by a Reforming mob in 1559, and the existing church is probably built on the site. There are carved fragments in the church, including the stone effigy of an abbot, and another of a knight.

Access at all reasonable times.

Crail Parish Church

[38 (G6)] On A917, Marketgate, Crail, Fife. (NGR: NO 614080 LR: 59)

The substantial aisled church, dating from the 13th century, with a tower and spire at the west end, was raised to collegiate status by William Myrton in 1517. It was dedicated to St Maelrubha and St Mary. The church was altered in later centuries, including restoration in 1963, and the chancel has been reduced in length. The church houses a weathered Pictish stone, with interlace and carvings of figures and animals, and 17th-century carving. There is an interesting burial ground with fine monuments (including to the Lumsdens, Bruces and Moncrieffs) and a mort-house, and a museum in Crail.

Sales area. WC. Disabled access. Parking nearby.

Open Jun-mid Sep, 14.00-16.00.

Cramond Kirk

[39 (H5)] Off A90, Cramond Glebe Road, Edinburgh. (NGR: NT 190709 LR: 66)

Set in the picturesque village of Cramond with its white-washed buildings, the body of the fine kirk was rebuilt in 1656 and altered in later centuries, while the crenellated tower dates from the 15th century. The church was dedicated to St Columba. There is a fine hammerbeam roof, a bell of 1619, and an interesting burial ground. The remains of the Roman fort are behind the kirk, and there is an exhibition about Cramond village in the Maltings.

Plan of kirkyard available. WC. Disabled access. Parking nearby.

Open during Edinburgh Festival, daily 14.00-17.00; services Sun 9.30/ 1100.
Tel: 0131 336 2036   Fax: 0131 336 2036
Web: www.cramondkirk.org.uk   Email: cramond.kirk@cwcom.net

Crathie Parish Church

[40 (E5)] On A93, 6 miles W of Ballater, Kincardineshire. (NGR: NO 265949 LR: 44)

Overlooking the scant ruins of an earlier church, dedicated to St Monirus, and the River Dee, the present building is cruciform in plan, with a square tower crowned by a spire. It was started in 1893, and Queen Victoria laid the foundation stone. The church is used by the Royal Family when staying at nearby Balmoral. John Brown, Victoria's manservant, is buried in old Crathie graveyard. *Parking.*

Open Apr-Oct, Mon-Sat 9.30-17.00, Sun 12.45-17.00.

Crichton Collegiate Church

[41 (H6)] Off B6367, 2 miles E of Gorebridge, Midlothian. (NGR: NT 381616 LR: 66)

In a pleasant location near the magnificent ruin of Crichton Castle, the solid and impressive collegiate church was founded by William Crichton, Lord Chancellor of Scotland, in 1449 on an earlier site, and dedicated to St Mary and St Mungo. Fine pointed barrel vaults survive over the choir and transepts, and the square tower over the crossing.

The tower has a corbelled-out parapet, and there are grotesque stone faces survive around the edge of the roof. There is no nave, and the building was restored in 1898. The burial ground has interesting memorials. Crichton Castle is open to the public.

WC. Disabled access. Parking.

Open May-Sep, Sun afternoons or by appt.

Tel: 01875 320364
Fax: 01875 320508

Cross Kirk, Peebles (HS)

[42 (H5)] On A703, Cross Road, Peebles, Borders. (NGR: NS 250407 LR: 73)

A large cross and inscribed stone were found here in 1261, and Alexander III established a church called Cross Kirk. This was elevated to a Trinitarian friary

(Red Friars), founded about 1474 and dedicated to St Nicholas. It was a place of pilgrimage. The church was used by the parish from 1561 until 1784, after which it became ruinous. Much of the late 13th-century church survives, consisting of the tower, nave, chancel, sacristy, and later burial aisles.

Nothing remains of the 12th-century church of St Andrew, also used as a collegiate church [NT 246405], except the tall restored tower. It was burned by the English in 1548, and there are some interesting markers in the burial ground.
Parking nearby. Disabled access.
Access at all reasonable times.

Crosshall Cross

[43 (H6)] On B6461, 5 miles NE of Kelso, 0.5 miles N of Eccles, Crosshall, Borders.
(NGR: NT 760422 LR: 74)
The ten-foot carved cross has a round head, and is decorated on all four sides, including with crosses, a rough figure and a hound.
Disabled access. Parking nearby.
Access at all reasonable times.

Crossraguel Abbey (HS)

[44 (I4)] Off A77, 2 miles SW of Maybole, Ayrshire. (NGR: NS 275084 LR: 70)
The large and well-preserved ruin of a Cluniac abbey, founded by Duncan, Earl of Carrick, in 1216, and dedicated to St Mary. The name is from 'Cross at Riaghail', believed to be a reference to St Regulus (Rule), and suggesting this is an older site. The abbey was attacked in 1306 during the Wars of Independence, and was rebuilt although the church lost its transepts. Although dissolved during the Reformation, there were monks here until 1592. Allan Stewart, Commendator of the abbey, was roasted 'in sop' until he signed over the abbey lands to the Kennedys. Impressive remains survive of the church, cloister, chapter house, gatehouse, abbot's tower and many of the domestic buildings. There are many grave slabs, some finely carved.
Exhibition on medieval building techniques. Sales area. WC. Picnic area.
Car and coach parking. £.
Open Apr-Sep, daily 9.30-18.30; last ticket sold 18.00.
Tel: 01655 883113

Cullen Old Kirk

[45 (D6)] Off A98, 0.75 miles SW of Cullen town centre, Aberdeenshire.
(NGR: NJ 507663 LR: 29)
The 'interior parts' of Elizabeth de Burgh, wife of Robert the Bruce, were buried at Cullen, after she died here, and Robert founded a chaplaincy in 1327. It was raised to a collegiate church in 1543 by Alexander Ogilvie, was dedicated to St

Mary although the original dedication appears to have been to St Nechtan, and is still used as a parish church. The fine cruciform church has a 13th-century nave, south transept of 1539 (St Anne's Aisle), and north transept from the 18th century. It houses a 16th-century carved tomb and stone effigy of Alexander Ogilvie of Deskford, who died in 1554, and another for James Ogilvie, Earl of Seafield (and Chancellor of Scotland in 1707). There is also a laird's loft (the Seafield Loft) of 1602 and 17th-century box pews. The burial ground has many interesting markers, some finely carved.

Parking.

Open summer, Tue and Thu 14.00-16.00, or by appt.

Tel: 01542 841851

Culloden Well

[46 (D5)] Off B9006, 3.5 miles E of Inverness, Highland. (NGR: NH 723452 LR: 27)

Located in a forestry plantation along a trail, the spring flows into a covered stone basin housed in a round building. It was dedicated to St Mary. It was a healing and clootie well, and rags, clothing and threads were (and are) left on surrounding trees.

Access at all reasonable times – walk to well.

Culross Abbey (HS)

[47 (H5)] Off B9037, 6.5 miles W of Dunfermline, Kirk Street, Culross, Fife.
(NGR: NS 989863 LR: 65)

St Serf had a monastery here, and it was to Culross that St Enoch came, pregnant with St Mungo (Kentigern). Mungo was educated here by Serf, and Culross became a place of pilgrimage. The abbey, dedicated to St Serf and St Mary, was founded in 1217 by Malcolm, Earl of Fife, as a Cistercian establishment on the site of a Culdee community.

Most of the buildings are ruinous, except the choir of the abbey church and tower, which were used by the parish since 1633. The church was altered in 1824 and restored in 1925. In the church is the tomb, carved effigy and memorial of Sir George Bruce of Carnock (who is associated with the nearby Palace) and his family. The ruins are also open to the public. There are fragments of three cross shafts near the church, dating from the 8th or 9th century.

Culross is a picturesque place with white-washed buildings, and located here is the historic and interesting Culross Palace (which is in the care of The National Trust for Scotland and open to the public).

Sales area. WC. Disabled access. Parking nearby.

Ruins open all year at reasonable times; parish church open summer, daily 10.00-dusk, winter daily 10.00-16.00.

Dalmeny Parish Church

[48 (H5)] Off B924, 8 miles NW of Edinburgh, Lothian. (NGR: NT 144775 LR: 65)

The fine and largely unaltered Romanesque church, dating from about 1130, has a rectangular nave, a rib-vaulted square chancel with rounded apse, and a modern square tower, as well as the 17th-century Rosebery Aisle. It was dedicated to

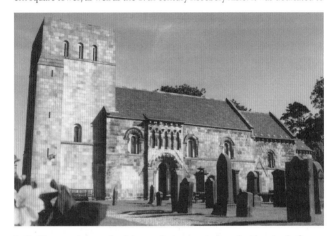

St Cuthbert, and the arch of the south doorway is carved with animals, figures and grotesque heads. There is further carving in the church, and a historic burial ground.

WC. Disabled access. Parking nearby. Donations welcome.

Open Apr-Sep, Sun 14.00-16.30 – key available from manse or post office, 5 Main Street at times outwith above. Coach parties should tel in advance.

Tel: 0131 331 1479

Deer Abbey (HS)

[49 (D6)] Off A950, 9 miles W of Peterhead, Aberdeenshire. (NGR: NJ 968482 LR: 30)

St Drostan is said to have founded a monastic community at Deer (probably at Old Deer), as early as 520 (although 580 and 719 are also given), and it was here that the famous 9th-century Book of Deer was written. This was acquired by Cambridge University Library in 1715, although only rediscovered in 1860.

A Cistercian abbey was founded in 1219 by William Comyn, Earl of Buchan, and dedicated to the Blessed Virgin Mary, although on a different site from Drostan's. Comyn was buried here. The lands passed in 1587 to Robert Keith, Lord Altrie. His nephew, Robert Keith of Benholm, seized the abbey in 1590, and was only ejected by the Earl Marischal with 40 men. The ruins of the church are fragmentary, after having been reduced in the 19th century to build a mausoleum, but the infirmary, Abbot's House and south cloister range are better preserved.

Parking.

Access at all reasonable times.

Tel: 01466 793191

Deskford Church (HS)

[50 (D6)] Off B9018, 4 miles S of Cullen, Aberdeenshire. (NGR: NJ 509616 LR: 29)

The medieval church, now ruinous, was rectangular in plan and dedicated to St John. There is a finely carved sacrament house of 1551, which was provided by Alexander Ogilvie of Deskford and Elizabeth Gordon, his wife (who are both buried at Cullen Old Kirk), as well as a monument to William Ogilvie.

Access at all reasonable times.

Tel: 01466 793191

Dornoch Cathedral

[51 (C5)] Off A949, Castle Street, Dornoch, Sutherland. (NGR: NH 797896 LR: 21)

There was probably an early monastery at Dornoch, referred to in the 12th cen-

tury, and founded by St Finbar in the 7th century. The cathedral was established in 1233 by Gilbert de Moravia, Bishop of Caithness from 1233-46, and dedicated to the Blessed Virgin Mary. Gilbert was made a saint, and is buried in the cathedral. There is also the damaged stone effigy of Sir Richard de Moravia, brother of Gilbert.

The cathedral is cruciform in plan and has a central crenellated tower and spire. The chancel and crossing piers date from the 13th century, although the aisles of the nave have gone. The church stands in an old burial ground (in 1761 the minister complained that pigs, which roamed freely in the graveyard, were digging up and eating buried corpses). The cathedral was torched in 1570 by the Mackays of Strathnaver, and the transepts and choir were not reroofed until 1616. The nave was rebuilt and the rest of the building restored in the 19th century, and there are fine modern stained glass windows. The exterior has many gargoyles, some of them dating from the 13th century.

Opposite the cathedral is the Bishop's Palace, now the Dornoch Castle Hotel.
Explanatory boards. WC. Disabled access. Parking.
Open all year, 9.00-dusk.
Tel: 01862 810357/296

Dryburgh Abbey (HS)

[52 (H6)] Off B6356 or B6404, 8 miles SE of Melrose, Borders. (NGR: NT 591317 LR: 73)
There may have been an early monastery, associated with St Modan, who was believed to have been abbot in 622. The abbey was founded by David I as a Premonstratensian (White Canons) establishment in 1150, and dedicated to St Mary. The Abbey was burnt by the English in 1322, 1385 and 1544, although it was occupied by monks until at least 1584. The ruins stand in an outstanding picturesque location near the River Tweed. Most of the buildings date from the 12th and 13th centuries, and part of the church survives, as does the cloister,

including the fine chapter house, parlour and vestry. Sir Walter Scott and Earl Haig are buried at Dryburgh.

Gift shop. WC. Picnic area. Disabled access. Car and coach parking. Group concessions. £.

Open all year: Apr-Sep, daily 9.30-18.30; Oct-Mar, Mon-Sat 9.30-16.30, Sun 14.00-16.30, last ticket 30 mins before closing; closed 25/26 Dec and 1/2 Jan.

Tel: 01835 822381

Duddingston Kirk, Edinburgh

[53 (H5)] Off A199, Old Church Lane, Duddingston. (NGR: NT 284726 LR: 66)

In the pretty village of Duddingston on the edge of Holyrood Park, the fine old church dates from the 12th century, although altered in later centuries, including the addition of the north aisle. The old entrance of the church has a fine Romanesque arch with interesting carvings, including Christ on the Cross. There is a watchtower (to deter bodysnatchers), 17th-century jougs, and fine gardens.

Sales area. Refreshments. WC. Disabled access. Parking nearby.

Open Jun-Sep, Sat 11.00-17.00, Sun 14.00-17.00.

Dunblane Cathedral (HS)

[54 (G5)] Off B8033, 5.5 miles N of Stirling, Stirlingshire. (NGR: NN 782015 LR: 57)

Dunblane is associated with St Blane, who is said to have been given a dun or fort here, by the banks of the Allen River, in the 6th century. There was an early monastery here, and the bell tower dates from the 11th century. The present

lofty cathedral is mostly 13th century and consists of an aisled nave, choir and bell tower. The choir continued to be used, while other parts became ruinous after the Reformation. The building was restored in 1889-93, and is used as the parish church. There is fine carving within the church, medieval stalls, and a 9th-century ringed cross-slab and second carved stone.

A brass memorial in the floor of the choir commemorates the poisoning of Margaret Drummond and her sisters. Margaret is said to have been the lover (or wife) of James IV, and she was murdered so he could marry Margaret Tudor.

Dunblane is a picturesque place, and the Cathedral Museum is housed in barrel-vaulted chambers, dating from the 17th century, and displays include paintings, artefacts and books that chart the history of the Cathedral from the 6th century to 1893. There is also a large collection of communion tokens.

Sales area. WC. Disabled access. Parking nearby.

Open all year.
Tel: 01786 823338

Dundrennan Abbey (HS)

[55 (J5)] On A711, 6 miles SE of Kirkcudbright, Dumfries and Galloway.
(NGR: NX 749475 LR: 83)
The abbey was founded in 1142 by David I and Fergus, Lord of Galloway, as a Cistercian establishment dedicated to the Blessed Virgin Mary. Mary, Queen of Scots, stayed here on 15-16 May 1568, her last night on Scottish soil before escaping to England. The last Abbot died in 1605, and the east end of the abbey church was used by the parish until 1742, while the rest became ruinous.

Parts of the church (particularly the transepts), chapter house and cloister survive. There are several carved grave slabs, tombs and the stone effigy of an abbot.

Sales area. Disabled access. Car and coach parking. Group concessions. £.

Open Apr-Sep, daily 9.30-18.30; Oct-Mar wknds only, Sat 9.30-16.30, Sun 14.00-16.30; last ticket 30 mins before closing; closed 25-26 Dec and 1-2 Jan.
Tel: 01557 500262

Dunfallandy Stone (HS)

[56 (F5)] Off A9, 1 mile S of Pitlochry, Perthshire. (NGR: NN 944564 LR: 52)
A magnificent Pictish cross-slab, moved in the late 19th century from the old chapel at Killiecrankie to its present location outside Dunfallandy House. The front has a beautifully carved full-length cross with spirals, knotwork and bosses, and surrounding carving includes two four-winged angels and a sea monster with human legs in its jaws. The back is framed by two fish-tailed serpents, holding a human head in their jaws, and is decorated with symbols and carving.

Access at all reasonable times – stone is enclosed in a glass case for protection – viewing may be difficult in wet weather.

Dunfermline Abbey (HS)

[57 (H5)] Off A994, Monastery Street, Dunfermline, Fife. (NGR: NT 089872 LR: 65)

Dunfermline was an important Pictish centre, and there was a palace of the early Scottish kings. The abbey was founded about 1070 by St Margaret, wife of Malcolm Canmore (they were married near here), as a Benedictine house, dedicated to the Holy Trinity. Margaret was made a saint, and she and Malcolm were buried here. Dunfermline became a major centre of pilgrimage, and St Margaret's Cave is nearby (see separate entry). Abbot House (Maygate, Dunfermline) has information on the abbey, as well as the recreated shrine of St Margaret.

At the Reformation, the last abbot George Durie was responsible for removing Margaret's and Malcolm's remains to the continent, and the Jesuits of Douai in Spain acquired her head. Robert the Bruce's body (apart from his heart, which is interred at Melrose Abbey) was entombed before the high altar, and other kings and queens are also said to have been buried here, including David I. The Abbey

was sacked in 1560, and fell into disrepair and ruin, although part of the church continued to be used, and was restored and rebuilt in modern times: the medieval nave survives, while the adjoining parish church, occupying the site of the choir, is 19th century.

The ruins of the royal palace (birthplace of David II, James I and Charles I) stand nearby, which was developed from the guest range of the abbey, and the

Dunglass Collegiate Church (see next page)

church, domestic buildings of the abbey, and remains of the palace are open to the public.

Explanatory displays. Gift shop. Parking nearby. Group concessions. £.

Open Apr-Sep, daily 9.30-18.30; Oct-Mar, Mon-Wed and Sat 9.30-16.30, Thu 9.30-12.00, Sun 14.00-16.30, closed Fri; last ticket 30 mins before closing; choir of abbey church open Mon-Sat 10.00-16.30, Sun 14.00-16.30.

Tel: 01383 739026 (HS)/01383 872242 (church)   Fax: 01383 739026

Dunglass Collegiate Church (HS)

[58 (H6)] Off A1, 6.5 miles SE of Dunbar, Berwickshire. (NGR: NT 766718 LR: 67)

The empty but almost complete church of St Mary, cruciform in plan, with a square central tower, and vaulted and stone-slabbed roof. It was founded about 1450 as a college of canons by Sir Alexander Home, whose castle was nearby but which has now gone after being blown up by gunpowder. The church was held against English raiders in 1544, but by the 18th century was being used as a barn.

Parking nearby.

Access at all reasonable times.

Dunkeld Cathedral (HS)

[59 (G5)] Off A9, Dunkeld, Perthshire. (NGR: NO 025426 LR: 52)

Dunkeld, on the banks of the Tay, was an important royal site in Pictish times, and in the cathedral is a large weathered Pictish cross-slab. There was probably an early monastic and Culdee community here, and some of the relics of St Columba were brought to Dunkeld after Iona was abandoned in the 9th century because of Norse raids. The cathedral was dedicated to St Columba.

Although partly ruinous, this is an imposing building in a wooded setting. The 14th-century choir of the cathedral is still used as the parish church, while the aisled nave, with a large tower at the north-west corner, is ruinous. The 15th-century chapter house, off the choir, has a small museum.

The splendid tomb and stone effigy of Alexander Stewart (d. 1405), Wolf of Badenoch, is located in the choir, and there is also the effigy and tomb of Bishop William Sinclair (d. 1337) and Bishop Cardney (d. 1437). Fine window tracery survives, and the vaulted ceiling of the ground floor of the tower has painted biblical scenes. There are also several cross-slabs. The tower, ruined nave and south porch are in the care of Historic Scotland.

Explanatory displays. Cathedral shop. Picnic area. Disabled access. WC and Parking nearby. Donations welcome.

Ruined nave and tower open all year; choir used as parish church: open Apr-Sep, Mon-Sat 9.00-18.30, Sun 14.00-18.30; Oct-Mar, Mon-Sat 9.30-16.00, Sun 14.00-16.00; closed New Year's Day.

Tel: 01350 727688   Fax: 01350 727688

Dupplin Cross (HS)

[60 (G5)] On B8062 or B934, 5 miles E of Auchterarder, St Serf's Church, Dunning, Perthshire. (NGR: NO 019146 LR: 15)

The magnificent cross formerly stood at Cross Park Field, near to the site of the ancient palace at Forteviot, but is now housed in St Serf's Church at Dunning. It is a free-standing cross, some six feet high, and dating from the 9th or 10th century. The cross has interlace knotwork, scrolled designs, and one panel contains a Latin inscription, translated as CU [...]NTIN FILIUS FIRCUS, believed to be for Constantine MacFergus, a Pictish king at the end of the 8th century, who ruled over both Picts and Scots.

Housed in St Serf's Church, Dunning: see separate entry.

Durisdeer Church

[61 (I5)] Off A702, 6 miles NE of Thornhill, Durisdeer, Dumfries and Galloway. (NGR: NS 897037 LR: 78)

The church, cruciform in plan and dating from 1699, houses the Queensberry Marbles, the stunning stone recumbent effigies, in black and white marble, of the 2nd Duke and Duchess of Queensberry. The tomb dates from 1711, and is in a burial aisle occupying one 'arm' of the church. In the vault below are 29 lead coffins containing the remains of the Douglas family. There is also a Martyr's Grave of 1685 from the troubled Covenanting period, and other fine monuments in the burial ground.

The Well Path runs through the village, a Roman road later used as a pilgrimage route to Whithorn.

The fabulous Drumlanrig Castle is nearby.

Parking.

Open all year.

Eassie Carved Stone (see next page)

Eassie Carved Stone and Church (HS)

[62 (G6)] Off A94, 6 miles W of Forfar, Eassie Church, Angus. (NGR: NO 353474 LR: 54)
The church, which was dedicated to St Fergus and rebuilt in the 16th century, stands in an irregularly shaped burial ground, indicating an ancient site. Located in the ruins is a grand Pictish cross-slab, which has a full-length cross with interlaced designs. It is also decorated with four-winged angels (the top right is damaged), and a huntsman, stag, and perhaps hunting dog. On the other side is a Pictish beast above a double disc and z-rod; three robed figures; and other carvings. The stone has recently been cleaned, and is encased in glass for protection.
Parking nearby
Access at all reasonable times.

Edderton Cross-Slab

[63 (D4)] Off A836, 5 miles NW of Tain, 0.5 miles E of crossroads at Edderton, Ross and Cromarty, Highland. (NGR: NH 719842 LR: 21)
Standing in the burial ground of the 18th-century Edderton Free Church is a carved Pictish cross-slab, although it now leans. On one side is a cross, below which is a rider within a curved frame, while on the other side is a large ringed cross with a tall shaft. There are the ruins of an earlier church to the east of the later building. Edderton was the site of an abbey, founded by Farquhar, Earl of Ross, in the 1220s, but this was soon moved to Fearn (see separate entry). The first names of trees and shrubs in the kirkyard spell 'Eader Dun' (Edderton).
Disabled access. Parking nearby.
Cross-slab: access at all reasonable times; church open by appt.
Tel: 01862 812245 (Edderton Old Church Trust)

Edrom Church (HS)

[64 (H6)] Off A6105, 3.5 miles NE of Duns, Berwickshire. (NGR: NT 827558 LR: 67)
The present church mostly dates from 1732, with alterations in 1886, although it incorporates the much altered Blackadder Aisle of 1499. It replaced an earlier church, dating from the 12th century, and dedicated to St Mary. The richly carved Romanesque doorway from this old church, built by Thor Longus about 1105, has been reused in a burial vault to the west of the present building.
Car parking.
Access at all reasonable times.

Eileach an Naoimh (HS)

[65 (G3)] N of Jura, one of the Garvellach islands. (NGR: NM 640097 LR: 55)
St Brendan founded a monastery on the picturesque island in 542, and there are the remains of churches, beehive cells, other buildings and burial grounds. Eithne, St Columba's mother, is said to be buried here, her grave marked by a

setting of stones, and there is also a spring: the well of St Columba. The island can be reached by hired boat from Toberonochy on the island of Luing, weather permitting.

Access at all reasonable times – subject to weather.

Eilean Mor, South Knapdale

[66 (H3)] E of Jura, 2 miles W of the mainland at Kilmory, Eilean Mor.
(NGR: NR 665755 LR: 61)

Standing on the island, which is owned by the SNP, is a fine but broken cross [NR 667753] with interesting carvings, and said to mark the burial of St Cormac. The remains of a chapel [NR 666752], with a barrel-vaulted chancel, are nearby. The chapel was dedicated to St Cormac, appears to date from the 13th century, and there is a stone effigy of a priest. A cave [NR 667753] is also associated with the saint.

Elgin Cathedral (HS)

[67 (D5)] Off A96, North College Street, Elgin. (NGR: NJ 222632 LR: 28)

Once one of the most impressive churches in Scotland, and second in size only to St Andrews, the cathedral is now a magnificent and picturesque ruin. The building was cruciform in shape with a central tower, has two large towers at the west end, and both the nave and choir had aisles. There is a fine octagonal vaulted chapter house, as well as a Pictish cross-slab, the large stone effigy of a bishop, and table tombs in the interesting burial ground.

The building dates from the 13th century, and was founded in 1224 as the seat of the

Bishops of Moray, after they removed from Spynie, on the site of a church dedicated to the Holy Trinity. The Cathedral was torched by Alexander Stewart, Wolf of Badenoch, in 1390 as the then bishop had excommunicated him. The church was repaired, but deteriorated after the Reformation: the central tower collapsed in 1711, bringing down much of the nave and transepts.

The Bishop's Palace at Spynie, a hugely impressive fortress, is also open, and there is a museum in Elgin.

Explanatory displays. Gift shop. Disabled access. Parking nearby. £. Joint entry ticket for Spynie Palace available (£).

Open all year: Apr-Sep, daily 9.30-18.30; Oct-Mar, Mon-Wed and Sat 9.30-16.30, Thu 9.30-12.00, Sun 14.00-16.30, closed Fri; last ticket 30 mins before closing; closed 25/26 Dec and 1/2 Jan.

Tel: 01343 547171

Eynhallow Church (HS)

[68 (A5)] S side of island of Eynhallow, W of Rousay, Orkney. (NGR: HY 359288 LR: 6)

Eynhallow means 'Holy Isle', and there was probably an early monastery here. The church, dating from the 12th century, has a rectangular nave, with a porch at one end, and a square-ended chancel. The building was latterly used as a house, and it was not realised it was actually a church until 1854 when the island was evacuated because of fever.

Access at all reasonable times – access is by private boat hire.

Tel: 01856 841815

Falkirk Old and St Modan's Parish Church

[69 (H5)] Off A803, Manse Place (off High Street), Falkirk. (NGR: NS 887800 LR: 65)

St Modan is believed to have founded a church here in the 6th century. The large impressive church (the 'Spotted (Fail) Kirk') dates from the 12th century, although it was substantially rebuilt in 1738 and 1811 and was refurbished in the 1960s. The central tower is 16th century, and is crowned by a later octagonal belfry with 13 bells.

There is a 12th-century sanctuary cross, and two stone effigies, one for Alexander Livingston, who died in 1467, as well as two large modern stained glass windows.

In the burial ground are markers for some of those slain at the Battle of Falkirk in 1297 (when William Wallace was defeated by Edward I of England), including Sir John Graham and Sir John Stewart of Bonkyl: William Wallace is said to have carried Graham's body from the battlefield to the church for burial.

Refreshments. WC. Disabled access. Parking nearby.

Open Mon-Fri, 12.00-14.00.

Fearn Abbey

[70 (D5)] Off B9166, 5 miles SE of Tain, Hill of Fearn, Highland. (NGR: NH 837773 LR: 21)

The large solid church, dating from the 14th century and rectangular in plan, is all that survives of the abbey buildings, and is one of the oldest pre-Reformation Scottish churches still used for worship. Known as the 'Lamp of the North', the abbey was a Premonstratensian establishment, dedicated to St Augustine. It was founded by Ferquhard MacTaggart, Earl of Ross, around 1227 and moved here in 1238 from Edderton. Patrick Hamilton, Commendator from 1517, was burnt for heresy at St Andrews in 1528. The abbey church was rebuilt in 1772 (after the nave roof had collapsed in 1742 killing 44 people), and restored in 1972 and 2001. There is an interesting burial ground.

Sales area. WC. Disabled access. Parking.

Open May-Sep, Sat and Sun 10.00-16.30; other times tel for appt.

Tel: 01862 871247

Fortrose Cathedral (HS)

[71 (D5)] On A832, 6 miles NE of Inverness, Highland. (NGR: NH 727565 LR: 27)

Bishop Robert moved the cathedral of Ross from Rosemarkie to Fortrose between 1214 and 1249. The cathedral was dedicated to St Peter and St Curitan (Boniface), and a long rectangle in plan, with buttressed walls and a tower at the north-western corner. It was in reasonable condition in 1649, but it is then said that most of it was demolished by Cromwell in 1653 to build a fort at Inverness. Only the south aisle and the north choir range, housing the chapter house and

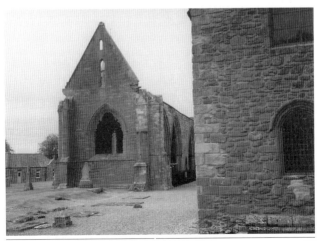

sacristy, survive, but the plan of the church is laid out in the grass. In the aisle are three arched tombs commemorating Euphemia, Countess of Ross, who was forced to marry the Wolf of Badenoch; Bishop Cairncross (d. 1545); and Bishop Fraser (d. 1507). Fortrose is a picturesque place and there is a walk (or drive) to Chanonry Point, viewpoint for dolphins and traditionally the site of the execution of Kenneth Mackenzie, the Brahan Seer.

Parking.

Access to ruins at all reasonable times.

Fowlis Easter Church

[72 (G6)] Off A923 or A90, 5 miles W of Dundee, Angus. (NGR: NO 323335 LR: 53)

The fine rectangular church, dedicated to St Marnon, probably dates from the 15th century, but is on a much older site. It was made into a collegiate establishment in 1454 by Lord Gray. It has many pre-Reformation features, including part of the original rood screen, large medieval board paintings of the Crucifixion, the Saints and St Catherine, alms dish, sacrament house and font.

Parking nearby. Donations welcome.

Open: on request (email william.horspool@tesco.net) or by key available from neighbouring houses.

Fowlis Wester Parish Church and Stone (HS)

[73 (G5)] Off A85, 5 miles E of Crieff, Perthshire. (NGR: NN 928240 LR: 52)

The rectangular church dates from the 13th century, was dedicated to St Bean, and although renovated in 1927, has many original features, including a leper's squint. There is a Pictish cross-slab, the Cross of Fowlis, over ten feet tall, under the north wall, while a replica stands on the original site in the village. One side of the stone has a tall cross with carved decoration; on the other are several horsemen, a double disc, and a group of figures, led by a man leading a cow, as well as other carving. The chain attached to the stone is probably the remains of jougs, to which petty criminals were attached for punishment. A second slab has a large ringed cross, filled with interlaced decoration, along with several carvings of saints.

Open by appt.

Tel 01764 683205.

Glamis Church, Pictish Stone and Well

[74 (G6)] Off A928, 5.5 miles SW of Forfar, Glamis, Angus. (NGR: NO 386468 LR: 54)

This is an early Christian site associated with St Fergus, who may have died about 750. There is a healing well situated below the church [NO 386470]: a trail, which has been landscaped, leads from the church. In the garden of Glamis Manse (across the road from the church) is a fine carved Pictish stone [NO 386469]. Fragments of other Pictish carved stones are housed in the modern church.

There was a church here from the 12th century or earlier, dedicated to St Fergus, but nothing remains except the south transept. This was used as the burial vault of the Earls of Strathmore, and built in 1459 by Isabella Ogilvie on the death of her husband, Patrick Lyon, Lord Glamis. The rest of the building was replaced by a new church in 1792. Glamis is home to the Angus Folk Museum, and Glamis Castle is nearby.

Parking nearby. Sales area nearby.

Church, carved stone and healing well open at all reasonable times.

Glasgow Cathedral (HS)

[75 (H4)] Off A8, Castle Street, centre of Glasgow. (NGR: NS 602655 LR: 64)

The cathedral is one of the finest buildings in Scotland, dating from the 13th century and having survived the Reformation. It is cruciform in plan with an

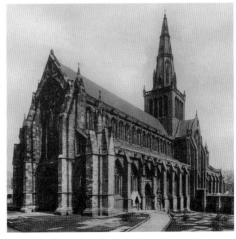

aisled nave and choir, short transepts, and a central tower and tall spire. Bishop Blackadder started the incomplete Blackadder Aisle on the south side of the church in the 15th century. The west end of the church was flanked by two towers, which were demolished in 1846 although it was intended to rebuild them: unfortunately money ran out. The building has a magnificent vaulted crypt (burial place of Mungo), a two-storey chapter house, and a 15th-century stone rood screen. There is much fine carving within the building.

The cathedral was dedicated to St Mungo, Glasgow's patron saint. The ring and the salmon form the basis of the city's coat of arms after Mungo had helped an unfaithful queen recover her ring from the fish. Mungo was active among the Britons of Strathclyde and founded a church here in 573. Glasgow is also associated with St Enoch or Thenew, Mungo's mother, and was a major centre of pilgrimage in medieval times. Near the cathedral is St Mungo Museum of Religious Life and Art, with fine art and objects from religion around the world.

Gift shop. Parking nearby.

Open all year: Apr-Sep, Mon-Sat 9.30-18.30, Sun 12.00-18.30; Oct-Mar Mon-Sat 9.30-16.30, Sun 14.00-16.30; closed 25/26 Dec & 1-2 Jan.

Tel: 0141 552 6891

Glenluce Abbey (HS)

[76 (J4)] Off A75, 1.5 miles N of Glenluce village, Galloway. (NGR: NX 185586 LR: 82)

The abbey was founded about 1192 by Roland, Lord of Galloway and Constable of Scotland, as a Cistercian establishment, dedicated to the Blessed Virgin Mary. It was visited by Robert the Bruce in 1329, by James IV on pilgrimage to Whithorn, and by Mary, Queen of Scots, in 1563. The abbey has also been associated with Michael Scott 'the Wizard', and thought by some to be where he is buried. The church and other buildings are ruinous, but the fine 16th-century chapter house is still roofed, and has fine window tracery and Green Men.

Explanatory panels.

Exhibition of finds. Shop. Refreshments. Disabled access. Car and coach parking. £.

Open Apr-Sep, daily 9.30-18.30; last ticket 18.00; Oct-Mar wknds only, Sat 9.30-16.30, Sun 14.30-16.30; last ticket sold at 16.00.

Tel: 01581 300541

Govan Old Parish Church

[77 (H4)] Off A739, 866 Govan Road, Govan, Glasgow. (NGR: NS 553658 LR: 64)

Govan is associated with St Constantine, and the church has a fine collection of early Christian stones, including a decorated sarcophagus (said to have held the relics of Constantine), five hogback tombstones, two cross shafts and upright crosses, and a number of recumbent slabs. The church, dedicated to St Constantine and dating from 1888, also has fine stained glass, a pipe organ and an interesting burial ground.

Sales area. WC. Parking nearby.

Open by arrangement only.

Tel: 0141 445 1941   Fax: 0141 401 7189

Web: www.govanold.org.uk

Greyfriars Kirk, Edinburgh

[78 (H5)] Greyfriars Place, near Museum of Scotland. (NGR: NT 258734   LR: 66)

There was a Franciscan friary near here, established in 1447 but ransacked by a Reforming mob in 1558. Nothing survives of it except the name 'Greyfriars'. The present Greyfriars Kirk, built in the garden of the friary, was the first post-Reformation church built in Edinburgh, and completed in 1620, although altered in the following centuries.

   The National Covenant was signed here in 1638, and a copy is on display. The historic kirkyard was used as a Covenanters' prison after the Battle of Bothwell Brig in 1679. It has many splendid old burial monuments dating from the 17th century onwards, and many well-known people are buried here, including William Adam and Sir George Mackenzie of Rosehaugh (Bloody Mackenzie).

   The memorial to Greyfriars Bobby is nearby – there is information and memorabilia about the wee dog in the church. It is a scandalous and unfounded rumour that Bobby survived by eating corpses from the graveyard.

Guided tours by arrangement. Visitor centre with explanatory displays and videos. Gift shop. WC. Disabled access and car parking. Parking nearby.

Open Apr-Oct, Mon-Fri 10.30-16.30, Sat 10.30-14.30; Nov-Mar, Thu 13.30-15.30; kirkyard open all year, 9.00-18.00.

Tel: 0131 225 1900/226 5429   Fax: 0131 225 1900

Email: greyfriarskirk@compuserve.com

Greyfriars, Kirkcudbright

[79 (J4)] Off A711, near MacLellan's Castle, Kirkcudbright, Dumfries and Galloway. (NGR: NX 683511   LR: 83)

A Franciscan friary was founded here in 1455 by James II, although the remains of the present church may date from the 13th century. Part of the building was remodelled in 1730, then fell into disuse, then became part of a school. The church was restored in 1922, but has an original piscina, holy water stoup and 17th-century dower chest, as well as the MacLellan Monument of 1597 with an effigy of a knight in armour. MacLellan's Castle (Historic Scotland) is nearby.

Parking nearby.

Access at all reasonable times.

Groam House Museum and Pictish Centre

[80 (D5)] On A832, 7 miles NE of Inverness, 1 mile NE of Fortrose, High Street, Rosemarkie, Highland. (NGR: NH 738575 LR: 27)

Rosemarkie was a major early Christian centre, and is associated with St Curitan or Boniface. St Moluag is said to have died here in 592, although his relics are believed to have been taken to Lismore (see Cathedral of St Moluag and Parish Church). The cathedral of Ross was located here, but later moved to nearby Fortrose (see separate entry). The award-winning museum has a good collection of Pictish carved stones, all found within the village, including the magnificent Rosemarkie Cross, a fine Pictish cross-slab. The museum also features audio-visual and static displays, activities and temporary exhibitions.

Guided tours on request. Exhibitions. Gift Shop. Disabled limited access and WC. Car and coach parking. Group concessions. £.

Open Easter week, then May-Sep, Mon-Sat 10.00-17.00, Sun 14.00-16.30; Oct-Apr Sat & Sun 14.00-16.00.

Tel: 01381 620961 (museum) 01381 621730 (office)   Fax: 01381 621730
Email: groamhouse@ecosse.net

Holyrood Abbey, Edinburgh (HS)

[81 (H5)] Edinburgh, by Holyrood Palace. (NGR: NT 269740 LR: 66)

The fine ruined church of an Augustinian abbey, founded by David I in 1128 after he had been saved from death at the antlers of a stag, survives beside the palace. The story goes that David was saved when a crucifix appeared and frightened off the stag. The abbey was, consequently, dedicated to the Holy Cross (Holy Rood).

The abbey was sacked in 1322 and 1385 by the English. David II, James V, and Henry Stewart, Lord Darnley, were all buried here. The English burnt the abbey and despoiled royal tombs in 1544 and 1547. The east end of the church was demolished during the Reformation, and the nave – the surviving portion – became the parish church. In 1672 it was made the Chapel Royal, but it was ransacked by an angry mob in 1688, and the roof collapsed in 1768. The most impressive part is the west facade, and one aisle is still roofed. Little survives of the rest of the abbey.

The Palace of Holyroodhouse is the official residence of the Queen in Scotland.

Holyroodhouse: Guided tours Nov-Mar. Gift shop. WC. Garden. Disabled access. Car and coach parking. Group concessions (10% groups of 15 or more). £££.

Open as Holyroodhouse: Open all year (except when monarch is in residence, Good Friday and 25/26 Dec): Apr-Oct, daily 9.30-17.15; Nov-Mar, daily 9.30-15.45.

Tel: 0131 556 1096/7371   Fax: 0131 557 5256

Web: www.royal-collection.gov.uk   Email: holyrood@royalcollection.gov.uk

Inchcolm Abbey (HS)

[82 (H6)] Inchcolm, 6.5 miles SE of Kirkcaldy, island in the Firth of Forth, Fife. (NGR: NT 191827 LR: 66)

The abbey, dedicated to St Columba, was founded in 1123 by Alexander I after he was washed up on Inchcolm and given refuge by a hermit (the hermit's cell survives), his boat having capsized crossing the Forth at Queensferry. The abbey was sacked by the English, including in 1542 and 1547. The picturesque abbey buildings, although ruined, are the best preserved monastic complex in Scotland, ranges around the cloister and the splendid chapter house being complete, and stands on a beautiful and interesting island.

Exhibition. Explanatory boards. Gift shop. Picnic area. WC. Disabled access. £ + ferry.

Open Apr-Sep, daily 9.30-18.30; ferry (£) (30 mins) from South or North Queensferry.

Tel: 0131 331 4857

Inchinnan Early Christian Stones and Church

[83 (H4)] Off A8, 3 miles N of Paisley, Renfrewshire. (NGR: NS 479689 LR: 64)

Inchinnan is associated with St Conval, who was active here in the 6th century, and it became a place of pilgrimage. The original church was a property of the Knights Templar from the 12th century, then the Knights Hospitaller after the Templars had been suppressed. The present church was built when the old church was demolished to make way for Glasgow airport, but incorporates some of the features. There is a carved sarcophagus, grave-slab and cross-slab in a covered area between the church and bell-tower.

Disabled access. Parking.

Access at all reasonable times; church open Thu during term time 12.00-13.30.

Inchkenneth Chapel (HS)

[84 (G2)] E side of Inch Kenneth, E side of Mull, Argyll. (NGR: NM 437354 LR: 47)

The fine ruinous church, dedicated to St Cainnech (or Kenneth, and hence the name of the island), dates from the 13th century and is rectangular in plan. There are 14th- and 15th-century carved grave slabs protected in the chapel, a 16th-century ring-headed cross of slate, and 17th- and 18th-century table grave slabs in the burial ground.

Access at all reasonable times.

Inchmahome Priory (HS)

[85 (G4)] Off A91, 4 miles E of Aberfoyle, Lake of Menteith, Stirlingshire.
(NGR: NN 574005 LR: 57)

This is one of the most beautiful of places, set on an idyllic wooded island in the picturesque loch. The site is dedicated to St Colman, and there was probably an early monastery here. The priory was founded in 1238 by Walter Comyn, 4th Earl of Menteith, as an Augustinian establishment. Robert the Bruce visited the priory, David II was married here, and Robert II also stayed here. Mary, Queen of Scots, was sent to Inchmahome for safety in 1547 before leaving for France. The chapter house is still roofed and houses a double stone effigy of Walter Stewart, Earl of Menteith (d. 1295), and his wife; another stone effigy; and there are other interesting grave slabs. A substantial part of the church also survives, including the carved west entrance. There is a ferry out to island from Port of Menteith.

Gift shop. Picnic area. WC. Parking (ferry). £.

Open Apr-Sep, daily 9.30-18.30; last ticket 18.00; ferry subject to cancellation during bad weather.

Tel: 01877 385294   Fax: 01877 385294

Innerpeffray Chapel

[86 (G5)] On B8062, 4.5 miles SE of Crieff, Perthshire. (NGR: NN 902183 LR: 58)

The church, a low rectangular building dedicated St Mary, was the original home of Innerpeffray Library and was used as the Drummond family burial place. A college was founded here by Lord Drummond about 1508, although there was a church here from 1342 or earlier. It retains the altar, and there is a Laird's Loft, reached by a turnpike stair. The chapel is in the care of Historic Scotland. The library, Scotland's oldest free lending library, was founded in 1680 by David, Lord Madderty, and is still open every day except Thursday. It is housed in a late 18th-century building, and has a notable collection of bibles, including one that was owned by the Marquis of Montrose, and rare books, including a translation of Vergil's *Aeneid*.

Sales area. Refreshments. Parking. &.

Library open all year: Mon-Wed & Fri-Sat 10.00-12.45 & 14.00-16.45, Sun 14.00-16.00; closed Thu; Oct-Mar, closes 16.00; Dec-Jan, by appt only; Chapel open all year except Thu & Sun.

Tel: 01764 652819/0131 668 8800 (chapel)

Iona Abbey (HS)

[87 (G2)] Off unlisted road, Iona, Argyll. (NGR: NM 287245 LR: 48)

Situated on the beautiful and atmospheric island of Iona, this is where St Columba came to form a monastery, and converted the northern Picts. Columba's shrine, within the Abbey buildings, dates from the 9th century. The abbey was abandoned after raids by the Norsemen, but was re-established by Queen Margaret, wife of Malcolm Canmore, in the 11th century. Some of the surviving abbey buildings date from the early 13th century after it had been refounded as a Benedictine establishment in 1203 by Reginald, son of Somerled, Lord of the Isles, dedicated to the Virgin Mary. The Abbey was used as a cathedral by the protestant Bishop of the Isles in the 17th century. Although the buildings became ruinous after the Reformation, the cruciform church, with a central tower, was rebuilt from 1899-1910, and the cloister was restored between 1938 and 1967 for the Iona Community, which welcomes guests to stay at the Abbey, and leads worship there each day.

The magnificent St Martin's Cross and St John's Cross (the latter a replica: the original is reconstructed and displayed in the Infirmary Museum) stand just outside the church, and the Infirmary Museum houses a splendid collection of carved stones and crosses, one of the largest collections of early Christian carved stones in Europe. The Black Stones of Iona were kept by St Martin's Cross and would reputedly turn black when somebody was lying. Between the abbey and the nunnery is MacLean's Cross, a fine 15th-century carved cross.

Many of the early Kings of Scots (and Lords of the Isles) are reputedly buried in 'Reilig Odhrain' Oran's cemetery by the 'Street of the Dead' – as well as kings of Ireland, France and Norway: 48 Scottish, 8 Norwegian and 4 Irish kings according to one 16th-century source. The 11th-century chapel of St Oran also survives, and may have been built on the orders of St Margaret. Among the kings buried here are said to be both Duncan and Macbeth.

The nearby Augustinian nunnery of St Mary was founded in 1208, also by Reginald, and is a fine consolidated ruin. There is a Sheila na Gig, much weathered, on one wall, and a museum in St Ronan's Chapel.

The Columba Centre at Fionnphort features an exhibition about the early church, Iona and St Columba, as well as having information on the local area.

Day tours from Oban in summer. Explanatory displays. Gift shop. Tearoom. WC. Picnic area. Parking at Fionnphort. £ (ferry). £ (admission).

St Martin's Cross, Iona

Open all year: Apr-Sep, daily 9.30-18.30; Oct-Mar, daily 9.30-16.30; last ticket 30 mins before closing – ferry from Fionnphort (£). Walk to abbey.

Jedburgh Abbey (HS)

[88 (16)] On A68, Jedburgh, Borders. (NGR: NT 650204 LR: 74)

The abbey was founded by David I about 1138 as an Augustinian establishment, dedicated to St Mary, although there had been a Christian community at Jedburgh from 830 or earlier. In 1285 Alexander III's marriage to Yolande de Dreux was consecrated here, but the abbey was attacked numerous times by the English, including in 1297, 1523 and 1544-5. The church continued to be used by the parish after the Reformation, until 1875 when the crown arch and vaulting of the crossing collapsed. Although unroofed, the church is in a good state of preservation. There is a fine rose window in the west front, and a richly carved Romanesque doorway. Remains or foundations of the domestic buildings of the abbey also survive on a terrace down to the river.

Visitor centre. Exhibition. Explanatory panels. Gift shop. Tearoom. Picnic area.
Limited disabled access and WC. Parking. £.
Open all year: Apr-Sep, daily 9.30-18.30; Oct-Mar, Mon-Sat 9.30-16.30, Sun
14.00-16.30; last ticket 30 mins before closing; closed 25/26 Dec and 1/2Jan.
Tel: 01835 863925

Keills Cross and Chapel (HS)

[89 (H3)] Off B8025, 6 miles SW of Tayvallich, Keills, Argyll. (NGR: NR 690806 LR: 55)
Keills was an important early Christian centre, and in the reroofed chapel, which
was dedicated to St Cormac, is the Keills Cross, which probably dates from the
8th century. The cross is carved with a central boss, panels of interlace, as well as
figures, and formerly stood just behind the chapel. There is a fine collection of
carved grave slabs protected in the chapel, most of them medieval.
Explanatory panels. Parking nearby.
Access at all reasonable times – short walk to chapel and may be muddy.

Kelso Abbey (HS)

[90 (H6)] Off A698, Kelso, Borders. (NGR: NT 729338 LR: 74)
Kelso was one of the richest monastic establishments in Scotland, yet it is much
more fragmentary than other Border abbeys. It was originally founded as a Tironensian abbey of the Blessed Virgin and St John in 1113 at Selkirk by the future
David I, but was moved here in 1138. James III was crowned at the abbey in 1460.
Much of the church and abbey were destroyed by the English in 1544-5, although
the establishment was not dissolved until 1560. The west transept was used as
the parish church, and little else remains, although the surviving part is very
impressive and this has been a very grand building.
Limited disabled access. Parking nearby.
Access at all reasonable times.

Kilarrow (Bowmore) Parish Church

[91 (H2)] On A846, Main Street, Bowmore, Islay.
(NGR: NR 312596   LR: 60)

The church, built by the Campbells of Shawfield in 1767, is unusual in being round in shape: so that there were no corners in which the devil could hide. The church can hold 500 people after a gallery was added in 1830.

Parking nearby.

Open all year, daily 9.00-18.00.

Kelso Abbey (see previous page)

Kilbrannan Chapel (HS)

[92 (H3)] Off B8001, 7 miles S of Tarbert, Skipness, Argyll. (NGR: NR 907577   LR: 62)

The ruins of a rectangular 13th-century church, dedicated to St Brendan, lie to the south-east of Skipness Castle (which is also open to the public). The church was probably abandoned in the 18th century. There are fine grave slabs in the interesting burial ground, and excellent views across to Arran.

Car parking (castle).

Access at all reasonable times: walk to Skipness, then to church which can be muddy.

Kilchoman Cross

[93 (H2)] Off B8018, 3 miles NW of Bruichladdich, Islay. (NGR: NR 214631   LR: 60)

In the burial ground is a fine eight-foot-high disc-headed cross, which was carved about 1500, and is similar in execution to that now at Campbeltown. One face has the depiction of the Crucifixion, with other figures including a horseman and knotwork decoration. In the base are cups and a stone. Wishes are said to be granted if the stone is turned in the holes in the correct order – towards the sun. There are several carved grave slabs and markers, dating from the 15th century, and a stone known as the Sanctuary Cross. The early 19th century church, now abandoned, replaced an earlier building, which was dedicated to St Kiaran.

Parking nearby.

Access at all reasonable times.

Kilbrannan Chapel (see previous page)

Kildalton Cross and Chapel (HS)

[94 (H3)] Off A846, 7 miles NE of Port Ellen, Kildalton, Islay. (NGR: NR 458508 LR: 60)

There may have been an early Christian monastery here, dedicated to St Catan, and there is a magnificent carved free-standing cross, dating from the 8th century, and carved from a single slab. The ringed cross has a representation of the Virgin and Child flanked by angels on one side, while the other has serpent and boss patterns with four lions around the central boss and biblical scenes. The remains of a Norse ritual killing are said to have been found beneath the cross when it was excavated in 1890. The small ruined chapel, dedicated to St John the Beloved, dates from the 12th or 13th century, and is a simple rectangular building. It houses several grave slabs, several with carvings of warriors, and there are more in the churchyard, dating from the 15th-17th centuries. The fine 15th-century Thief's Cross is nearby, set within railings.

Parking nearby.

Access at all reasonable times.

Kilmartin Carved Stones (HS) and Church

[95 (G3)] On A816, Kilmartin, Argyll. (NGR: NR 834988 LR: 55)

There is a fine group of carved grave slabs protected in the burial ground, and two free-standing crosses, one very weathered, which has a Christ figure, in the church. The church dates from 1835, and was remodelled in 1900, although it stands on an older site, dedicated to St Martin.

There are many fine Prehistoric burial cairns and standing stones in the Kilmartin area, as well as the Kilmartin House Museum of Ancient Culture and the old fortress of Dunadd, stronghold of the Scots.

Parking.

Access to churchyard at all reasonable time; church open Apr-Oct, daily 9.30-18.00.

Kilmory Knap Chapel (HS)

[96 (H3)] Off B8025, Kilmory Knap, 14 miles SE of Lochgilphead, Loch Sween, Argyll. (NGR: NR 703752 LR: 62)

The 13th-century chapel, which was dedicated to St Mary, has been reroofed. It houses MacMillan's Cross, a fine medieval carved cross which looks like a piece of modern art, and a collection of grave slabs, found in the burial ground and moved to the chapel for protection from the elements. Kilmory Knap is a tranquil place, and the impressive Castle Sween is off the road (through the caravan site) which goes down to the chapel.

Explanatory panel. Parking nearby.

Access at all reasonable times.

Kilmun Church

[97 (H4)] On A880, 6 miles N of Dunoon, NE shore of Holy Loch, Argyll. (NGR: NS 166821 LR: 56)

This is the site of an early monastery of St Munn. The present T-plan church mostly dates from 1841, and features fine stained glass windows and a water-powered organ; adjoining is the domed mausoleum of the Campbell Dukes of Argyll, built in 1794 and housing the remains of 14 dukes and duchesses.

The solid tower of a collegiate church, established by Sir Duncan Campbell in 1442, also survives, although it detached from the church. There are 18th-century markers (and the resting place of the first lady doctor) in the burial ground. *Guided tours. Gift shop. Tearoom. WC. Car and coach parking. Donations welcome.*
Open Apr-Sep, Tue-Thu 13.30-16.30; all other times by arrangement.
Tel: 01369 840342

Kilwinning Abbey (HS)

[98 (H4)] Off A737, 3 miles N of Irvine, Kilwinning, Ayrshire. (NGR: NS 303433 LR: 63)
St Wynnyn or Winning (and hence the name of the town), is said to have had a church here in 715 (or the 6th century).

The abbey was founded in 1162 by Hugh de Morville, High Constable of Scotland, as a Tironensian establishment dedicated to St Mary and St Wynnyn. Kilwinning was a place of pilgrimage, the abbey was sacked during the Wars of Independence, and James IV visited the relics of St Winning in 1507. Gavin Hamilton, the last abbot, was an opponent of John Knox and was slain near Restalrig in 1571.

The abbey had been attacked by reformers in 1561, although part of the church continued to be used by the parish until 1775, when it was mostly demolished and a new church built on the site. Fragments survive of the original 13th-century church, chapter house and cloister, while the present church was built in 1774, replacing a building of 1590.
Parking.
Abbey ruins: access at all reasonable times.
Abbey Church by appt (tel: 01294 552929).

Kincardine O'Neil Old Parish Church

[99 (E6)] About 7 miles W of Banchory, just S of A93, Kincardine O'Neil, Aberdeenshire. (NGR: NO 593995 LR: 44)
The site is associated with St Erchan. A well, dedicated to him, stands across the road from the church, and is now enclosed in a small building of 1858, although there is apparently no water.

The rectangular church was abandoned in 1862 and is now ruinous, formerly having a two-storey hospice at one end, which was founded in 1233 by Alan Durward. There is a 14th-century carved doorway and interesting old burial markers in the churchyard.
Access at all reasonable times.

King's College Chapel, Old Aberdeen

[100 (E7)] Off A92, College Bounds, N of Aberdeen. (NGR: NJ 940081 LR: 38)

The collegiate chapel was founded by William Elphinstone, Bishop of Aberdeen, in 1495 and dedicated to St Mary. It is a fine old building with buttressed walls and a striking tower and crown steeple. It has magnificent choir stalls of the 15th century and considered to be the best medieval woodwork in Scotland, and fine modern stained glass. There is a visitor centre, and St Machar's Cathedral is nearby.

Open by arrangement.

Tel: 01224 273325/272137

Kinkell Church (HS)

[101 (E6)] Off A96 and B993, 2 miles S of Inverurie. (NGR: NJ 785190 LR: 38)

The ruinous shell of a 16th-century church, dedicated to St Michael, which may have been a property of the Knights of Jerusalem. There is a fine sacrament house of 1524, as well as the carved grave slab of Gilbert de Greenlaw, who was killed at the bloody Battle of Harlaw in 1411.

Access at all reasonable times.

Tel: 01466 793191

Kinloss Abbey

[102 (D5)] Off B9089, 3 miles NE of Forres, Kinloss, Moray. (NGR: NH 965615 LR: 27)

The very ruinous remains of a formerly large Cistercian abbey, founded by David I in 1150, and dedicated to the Blessed Virgin Mary. Edward I and Edward III of England visited. Much of the stone was robbed in the 1650s for the building of a fort at Inverness. Parts of the transept of the church and sacristy remain, as does the ruin of the abbot's house. A burial ground surrounds the ruins.

Access at all reasonable times.

Kirk of Calder

[103 (H5)] On B7015, 12 miles W of Edinburgh, Main Street, Mid Calder, West Lothian. (NGR: NT 075675 LR: 65)

The parish church, dating from 1541 and dedicated to St John, is a long rectangular building, with choir, small tower and belfry, and later transepts: the nave was never built. It has fine modern stained-glass windows. The Sandilands , who built the church, were buried here, and there are interesting markers in the burial ground, dating from the 17th century. Famous visitors include John Knox, David Livingstone and James 'Paraffin' Young

Guided tours. Explanatory displays: information on four centuries of Scottish history. Gift shop. Tearoom. WC. Disabled access. Car and coach parking.

Open May-Sep, Sun 14.00-16.00.

Tel: 01506 880207   Web: www.kirkofcalder.com   Email: kirkofcalder@netscape.net

Kirk of St Nicholas, Aberdeen

[104 (E7)] Off A956, Back Wynd off Union Street, Aberdeen. (NGR: NJ 940062 LR: 38)
Known as the 'Mither Kirk' of Aberdeen, there has been a church here from early
times, dedicated to St Nicholas, and the crossing and transepts may date from
the 12th century. The church was divided in two after the Reformation, then
largely rebuilt. The East Kirk (chancel) dates from 1752, the West (nave) from
1834-7, then 1875-77; while the central tower and spire are of 1874, built after a
fire destroyed the old spire. The congregations were united in 1980. St Mary's
Chapel, in the crypt, survives from the 15th-century church, and Sir John Gordon, executed after the Battle of Corrichie in 1562, is interred here. There is also
fine 17th-century embroidery, the Chapel of the Oil Industry, and a carillon of 48
bells, the largest in the UK. The adjoining graveyard has many table-tombs and
memorials, dating from as early as the 17th century.
*Guided tours. Explanatory displays. WC. Disabled access and hearing induction loop
for the deaf. Car parking nearby.*
**Open May-Sep, Mon-Fri 12.00-16.00, Sat 13.00-15.00, except closed local
holidays; other times by appt.**
Tel: 01224 643494

Kirkmadrine Early Christian Stones (HS)

[105 (J4)] Off A716, 7 miles S of Stranraer, Galloway. (NGR: NX 080483 LR: 82)
Kirkmadrine was contemporary with Whithorn, and there are three pillar stones,
dating from the 5th century, one carved with a circled cross and Latin inscription
'Here lie the holy and chief priests, Ides, Viventius and Mavorius'. These are
displayed in the adapted porch of the 19th-century chapel. The site was dedi-
cated to St Medran of Muskerry. The MacTaggarts of Ardwell were buried here.
Disabled access. Parking nearby.
Access at all reasonable times.

Ladykirk

[106 (H6)] Off B6470, 5.5 miles NE of Coldstream, Borders. (NGR: NT 889477 LR: 74)
Ladykirk is dedicated to St Mary (Our Lady) who James IV believed had saved
him from drowning at the nearby ford, and he built the church about 1500. The
substantial building, cruciform in plan, has a tower and domed belfry at the west
end and a three-sided apse, and is only about 300 yards from the English border.
The church was vaulted in stone so that it could withstand fire, and has buttressed walls to take the weight. The Wardens of the Marches often met here to
sort out disputes, and in 1560 a peace treaty was signed at Ladykirk.
Car parking.
Access at all reasonable times.

Largs Old Kirk (HS)

[107 (H4)] Off A78, Bellman's Close, off High Street, Ayrshire. (NGR: NS 200594 LR: 63)
There may have been a church at Largs as early as 711, but the first definite
mention is in 1263. It was dedicated to St Columba, and rebuilt in 1812. It was
later demolished, and nothing remains except the altered north transept, the
Skelmorlie Aisle, a burial vault and loft built by the Montgomerys of Skelmorlie in
1636. There are a number of fine burial monuments, as well as a painted ceiling.
Open Apr-Sep, daily 14.00-17.00: keyholder Largs Museum, which is nearby.
Tel: 0131 668 8800 (HS)/01475 687081 (Largs Museum)

Lesmahagow Priory

[108 (H5)] Off M74, 4.5 miles SW of Lanark, Lesmahagow. (NGR: NS 814398 LR: 72)
The priory was founded in 1144 by David I as a Tironensian establishment, dedicated to St Maclou: his relics were held here. The priory was burned in 1335 by
the English, then again in 1561 during the Reformation. Little remains, although
the site has been cleared and excavated. The priory church was demolished in
1803, and replaced by the current building, which has stained glass, a display in
the chapter house, and a bell dated 1625.
Explanatory displays. Sales area. Refreshments. Parking nearby.
Church: open by appt; excavated site: open at all reasonable times.
Tel: 01555 892425/697 Web: www.lopc.org.uk

Lincluden Collegiate Church (HS)

[109 (I5)] Off A76, 1.25 miles N of Dumfries. (NGR: NX 967779 LR: 84)
A Benedictine nunnery was founded by Uchtred, son of Fergus, Lord of Galloway before 1174, but was converted to a collegiate establishment in 1389 by
Archibald, 3rd Earl of Douglas, after it had fallen into disrepute. It was dedicated
to St Mary. James IV visited on his way to Whithorn, the college survived until the
1590s, then was converted into a house. There is a fine stone effigy in a recessed
tomb of Margaret, daughter of Robert III and wife of Archibald, 4th Earl. Much of
the choir and south transept survive, as does the north domestic range.
Disabled access. Parking nearby.
Access at all reasonable times.

Lindores Abbey

[110 (G5)] On A913. 0.5 miles E of Newburgh, Lindores, Fife. (NGR: NO 244185 LR: 59)
The reduced ruins of a Tironensian abbey, founded in 1191 by David, Earl of
Huntingdon, and dedicated to St Mary, St Andrew and All Saints. It was attacked
in the 15th century, then again by reforming mobs in 1543 and 1559. There are
fragments of the church, bell-tower and other buildings.
Open: check locally.

Logie Old Kirk, Bridge of Allan

[111 (G5)] Off A91, 2.5 miles N of Stirling, Logie, Airthrey Castle, Bridge of Allan, Stirlingshire. (NGR: NS 815970   LR: 57)

The church, dedicated to St Serf, stands in an oval kirkyard, and there are two hogback grave stones dating from the 11th century. The present building mostly dates from 1784, although a church here is mentioned in 1178, and it is a picturesque ruin in a fine location by the Logie Burn.

Access at all reasonable times.

Magdalen Chapel, Edinburgh

[112 (H5)] 41 Cowgate, Edinburgh. (NGR: NT 258735   LR: 66)

Although easy to miss, tucked away in the Cowgate, this is one of the oldest buildings in the city, established in 1541 by Michael McQuhane and Janet Rhynd (his wife), and dedicated to St Mary Magdalene. There are rare medieval stained glass roundels in their original setting, as well as a bell and clock dating from the early 17th century.

The chapel was used as a guildhall by the Incorporation of Hammerman from 1552-1862, when it was taken over by the Protestant Institute of Scotland, then from 1965 by the Scottish Reformation Society.

Guided tours. Explanatory displays. Gift shop. WC. Disabled access. Parking nearby.
Open all year: Mon-Fri, 9.30-16.00; at other times by appt.
Tel: 0131 220 1450   Fax: 0131 220 1450

Maiden Stone, Chapel of Garioch (HS)

[113 (D6)] Off A96, 1 mile NW of Chapel of Garioch, 5 miles NW of Inverurie, Aberdeenshire. (NGR: NJ 704247   LR: 38)

A highly decorated but weathered tall Pictish cross-slab with a long cross and other carvings.

Parking nearby.
Access at all reasonable times.

Maybole Collegiate Church (HS)

[114 (I4)] Off A77, Maybole, Ayrshire. (NGR: NS 301098   LR: 76)

The church, dedicated to St Mary and dating from the 13th century, housed a college of priests, founded in 1384 (the oldest such establishment in Scotland) by John Kennedy of Dunure in the existing parish church of St Cuthbert. The chapel was abandoned in 1563, and the Kennedy family took over the sacristy as their burial vault. The south door has fine carving, and there is an interesting burial ground.

Parking nearby.
Access at all reasonable times.

Meigle Parish Church and Museum (HS)

[115 (G6)] On A94, 12 miles SW of Forfar, Meigle. (NGR: NO 287447 LR: 53)

There was an important early Christian monastery here, possibly established by monks from Iona in 606, possibly by St Ninian. Meigle Parish Church is built on the site. This church dates from 1870 after the medieval church, dedicated to St Peter, had burned down, but has a fine stone font and an interesting burial ground. Meigle is said to be the burial place of Guinevere (Vanora), wife of Arthur, one of the stones recording her death by being torn apart for adultery.

The nearby museum has some 30 Pictish cross-slabs and carved stones, one of the best collections of Dark Age sculpture in Western Europe. The stones were found at, or near, the old churchyard, and many are exquisitely carved.

Museum: Exhibition. Sales area. WC. Disabled access and WC. Parking nearby. £.

Church open by appt; Museum open Apr-Sep, daily 9.30-18.30; Oct-Nov, Mon-Sat 9.30-16.30; Sun 14.00-16.30; last ticket 30 mins before closing.

Tel: 01828 640278 (church)/01828 640612 (museum)

Melrose Abbey (HS)

[116 (H6)] Off A7 or A68, in Melrose, Borders. (NGR: NT 550344 LR: 73)

An elegant and picturesque ruin, the abbey was founded as a Cistercian establishment by David I about 1136, and dedicated to the Blessed Virgin Mary. The church is particularly well preserved, while the domestic buildings and the cloister are very ruinous. The abbey was sacked by the English in 1322, 1385 and 1545, after which it never recovered. It was dissolved at the Reformation, although the nave of the church was crudely vaulted and used as a parish church

from 1618 until 1810, when it was finally abandoned.

The heart of Robert the Bruce is buried in the nave, and many of the powerful Douglas family are also interred here.

The former commendator's house has an exhibition of carvings and other artefacts.

Visitor centre. Museum in former Commendator's House. Gift shop. Refreshments. WC. Disabled WC. Picnic area. Car and coach parking (£). Group concessions. £.

Open all year, daily 9.30-18.30; last ticket 18.00; closed 25/26 Dec & 1/2 Jan.

Tel: 01896 822562

Merkland Cross, Ecclefechan (HS)

[117 (I5)] Off M74, 6 miles SE of Lockerbie, Merkland Smithy, near Ecclefechan, Dumfries and Galloway. (NGR: NY 250721 LR: 85)

A fine carved and decorated cross, dating from the 15th century, with an octagonal shaft crowned by a head of four fleur-de-lys.

Parking nearby.

Access at all reasonable times.

Mortlach Parish Church

[118 (D5)] Off A941, Dufftown, Moray. (NGR: NJ 323392 LR: 28)

Set in an attractive situation above the Dullan Water, Mortlach was associated with St Moluag around 566, and, although the present rectangular church dates from the 11th or 12th century, it stands on the site of an early monastery. In 1016 the church was lengthened by three spears' length on the command of Malcolm II after a victory over the Norsemen, and the tall Battle Stone in the burial ground is said to commemorate the victory. The chancel survives from the medieval period, although the church was remodelled in 1826, 1876 and 1931. In one wall is the stone effigy and tomb of Alexander Leslie of Kininvie, who died about 1549, and there is a Pictish symbol stone, as well as a memorial to Alexander Duff of Keithmore and his wife, and other memorials and an interesting burial ground.

Explanatory displays. Induction loop. Car and coach parking. Donations welcome.

Open Easter-Oct, daily 10.00-16.00.

Tel: 01340 820268

Munlochy Well

[119 (D4)] Just S of A832, 5 miles N of Inverness, 0.5 miles NW of Munlochy, Black Isle, Highland. (NGR: NH 641537 LR: 26)

A strange and unusual place, Munlochy Well is a clootie or rag well and still in use. A spring issues from a round hole and runs down into a trough. The well is surrounded by many rags and articles of clothing, hung on the trees and fences around the site. The well was dedicated to St Curitan or Boniface in Christian times, who is also associated with Rosemarkie.

Rags or articles of clothing should not be take from the well as any misfortune or illness of the owner will transfer to the person taking the article.
Parking.
Access at all reasonable times.

Museum of Scotland, Edinburgh

[120 (H5)] Chambers Street, Edinburgh.
(NGR: NT 256732 LR: 66)
Among the many attractions of this magnificent museum is the Monymusk

Munlochy Well

Reliquary, the crosier of St Fillan, and many splendid carved stones from the early Christian and medieval period.
Museum. Multimedia study room. Gift shop. Audio guides. Tearooms. Roof-top restaurant. WC. Disabled access & WC. Parking nearby.
Open all year: Mon-Sat 10.00-17.00, Tue 10.00-20.00, Sun 12.00-17.00; closed Christmas day.
Tel: 0131 247 4422 Fax: 0131 220 4819 Web: www.nms.ac.uk Email: info@nms.ac.uk

Muthill Old Church and Tower (HS)

[121 (G5)] On A822, 3 miles S of Crieff, Muthill. (NGR: NN 869170 LR: 58)
There has been a church here from early times (possibly dedicated to St Patrick, and there is said to have been a Culdee foundation), and the roofed 70-foot-tall tower dates from the 12th (or 11th?) century. The church, mostly 15th century, had an aisled nave and aisleless chancel, but the chancel was abandoned and then completely demolished after the Reformation and the nave is now ruinous. There is an interesting burial ground. Muthill Village and Parish Museum is in the village: Muthill is pronounced 'Mew-thil'.
Parking nearby.
Access at all reasonable times.

Netherton Cross, Hamilton

[122 (H5)] Off A724, Strathmore Road, Hamilton Old Parish Church, Hamilton, Lanarkshire. (NGR: NS 723555 LR: 64)

The Netherton Cross, dating from the 10th or 11th century, is a free-standing stone cross, decorated on all four sides with figures, animals and cross-weave. It stands in the burial ground of Hamilton Old Parish Church, having been moved from Hamilton Low Parks in 1926.

There are also Covenanting memorials and other interesting markers in the burial ground

The present church, Greek cross in plan, was designed and built by William Adam in 1732-4, the only church designed by him. There are fine stained-glass windows. It replaced the old parish church, which was on another site.

Church: WC. Disabled access. Car and coach parking.

Church: open all year, Mon-Fri, 10.30-15.30, Sat 10.30-12.00, Sun after 10.45 service; evenings by appt.

Tel: 01698 281905   Web: office@hopc.fsnet.co.uk   Email: www.hopc.fsnet.co.uk

Nigg Cross-Slab (HS) and Old Parish Church

[123 (D5)] Off B9175, 7 miles S of Tain, Nigg. (NGR: NH 804717 LR: 21)

Housed inside Nigg Old Parish Church is the fine carved Pictish cross-slab, broken and with a section missing, which dates from the 8th or 9th century. One side is decorated with a large cross, filled with interlaced patterns, while the surround has elaborate boss patterns.

There was a church here from the 13th century and earlier, dedicated to St Fiacre, but it was substantially altered in 1626, 1729 and later, and is now T-plan. The church bell dates from 1624.

There are interesting memorials in the burial ground, including a 14th-century marker, a 17th-century box tomb, and the Cholera Stone, commemorating an epidemic in 1832.

Parking.

Open Apr-Oct, daily 10.00-17.00: key from the manse opposite.

Tel: 01862 832214 (Nigg Old Trust)

Nith Bridge Cross

[124 (I5)] Off A702, Thornhill, Dumfries and Galloway. (NGR: NX 868954 LR: 78)

The fine carved cross, some nine feet tall, is the most complete Anglian Cross in Scotland apart from the Ruthwell Cross. Carvings include animals and winged beasts.

Parking nearby.

Access at all reasonable times.

Old Steeple, Steeple Church and Dundee Parish Church

[125 (G6)] Off A90, Nethergate, Dundee. (NGR: NO 401301 LR: 54)

The Old Steeple, dating from the 15th century, is all that remains of the splendid medieval church of St Mary's, which was founded in 1198 and was one of the finest churches in Scotland. The tower is some 156 feet high, and has walls eight feet thick in places. There are fine views from the tower, and the mercat cross is nearby. The church was burned in 1296 by Edward I of England, and was damaged in 1385, 1641, 1651 when Cromwellian forces used it as a stable, and 1745. Part of it was restored by William Burn after a fire of 1841 destroyed a library of old books and charters, and part of the church. The site of the nave is occupied by the Steeple Church, while the chancel is Dundee Parish Church (St Mary's) and has fine stained-glass windows.

Parking nearby. £.

Old Steeple open all year: Apr-Sep, Mon-Sat 10.00-17.00, Sun 12.00-16.00; Oct-Mar, Mon-Sat 11.00-16.00, Sun 12.00-16.00; Steeple Church open Jul-Aug, Tue 10.00-13.00 and Sat 12.00-15.00; Dundee Parish Church open May-Sep, Mon, Tue, Thu and Fri 10.00-12.00.

Old Steeple: Tel: 01382 206790 Fax: 01382 206790 Email: admin@dundeeheritage@sol.co.uk

Oronsay Priory and Cross

[126 (H2)] Off unlisted road, W side of Oronsay. (NGR: NR 349889 LR: 61)

There was an early monastery here, and the island has been associated with St Oran, although this may be a confusion over the name. The priory was founded in the 14th century as a house of Augustinian canons by John, Lord of the Isles, and was dedicated to St Columba. There are good remains of the church, cloister and domestic buildings.

  The fine carved Oronsay Cross, dating from about 1510, has a crucified Christ figure and patterns of foliage, as well as the inscription: 'this is the cross of Colinus, son of Cristinus MacDuffie'. There are over 30 carved grave slabs in the Prior's House, and this was used as a burial place by the MacNeils and MacDuffies. There are several stone effigies.

Open all year – on tidal island: access by foot (long walk) or post-bus is regulated by tides: check locally.

Orphir Church (HS)

[127 (B5)] Off A964, 8 miles SW of Kirkwall, Orphir, Orkney. (NGR: HY 334044 LR: 6)

The remains of an unusual round church, dating from the 11th or 12th century, and said to have been based on the Church of the Holy Sepulchre in Jerusalem. The church was dedicated to St Nicholas, and probably started by Earl Haakon

Paulsson before 1122, whose hall – 'bu' – was nearby. The apse survives but the rest was demolished for the building of a later church, itself demolished in 1953. The Orkneyinga Saga Centre is nearby.

Car and coach parking nearby.

Access at all reasonable times.

Tel: 01856 841815

Paisley Abbey

[128 (H4)] Off A726 or A737, Paisley, Renfrewshire. (NGR: NS 486640   LR: 64)

There was an early monastery here, established by St Mirren. A Cluniac priory was founded in 1163 by Walter, son of Alan, Steward of Scotland, dedicated to St Mirren, St Mary the Virgin, St James and St Milburga. The priory became an abbey in 1219, but the present church dates mostly from the 14th century after it had been damaged during the Wars of Independence. The tower collapsed in 1553, destroying the choir, although the splendid cruciform church was rebuilt and restored in the 20th century. The church has a long choir, aisled nave, transepts and a central tower.

  The church houses a stone effigy, thought to be of Marjorie, daughter of Robert the Bruce and mother of Robert II; and the tomb of Robert III. The Barochan Cross, dating from as early as the 8th century and decorated with warriors and human figures, is also housed here. Some 12th-century carving of the life of St Mirren survives in St Mirin's Chapel. The abbey is now used as the parish church, and there is fine woodwork, stained glass and interesting memorials.

  Part of the cloister also survives, altered and modernised, and known as the Palace of Paisley. There is a good museum in Paisley.

Refreshments. Sales area. WC. Limited disabled access. Parking nearby.

Open all year: Mon-Sat 10.00-15.30.

Tel: 0141 889 7654   Fax: 0141 887 3929

Parish Church of St Cuthbert, Edinburgh

[129 (H5)] W end of Princes Street, 5 Lothian Road. (NGR: NT 247735   LR: 66)

St Cuthbert is said to have established a church here in the 7th century, and the present building is the seventh on the site. It was begun in 1894 although it incorporates a tower of 1790, and features stained glass, Renaissance-type stalls, and a marble communion table. Many well-known people are buried in the kirkyard, including Thomas de Quincy and Alexander Nasmyth, and there is a round watch-tower, which was built to discourage bodysnatchers.

Explanatory displays. Burial ground. Cafe nearby. Gift shop nearby. WC. Disabled access. Parking nearby.

Open May-Sep, Mon-Sat 10.00-16.00, Sun for worship.

Tel: 0131 229 1142

Pluscarden Abbey

[130 (D5)] Off B9010, 6 miles SW of Elgin. (NGR: NJ 142576 LR: 28)

This was originally a Valliscaulian priory (one of three in Scotland), founded by Alexander II in 1230, and dedicated to St Mary, St John the Baptist, and St Andrew. It was damaged during the Wars of Independence, then in 1390 may have been torched by Alexander Stewart, the Wolf of Badenoch, along with Elgin Cathedral. In 1454 it became a Benedictine house after it had fallen into disre-

pute, but the church and domestic buildings became ruinous after the Reformation. The abbey was refounded and rebuilt in 1948 as a Benedictine monastery, although the splendid abbey church has no nave. There are many old burial markers, modern stained glass, and much of the precinct wall survives.

Guided tours by arrangement. Gift shop. WC. Disabled facilities. Parking nearby.
Retreats (accommodation available).
Open all year – short walk: daily 4.45-20.30; shop 8.30-17.00.
Tel: 01343 890257 Fax: 01343 890258
Web: monks@pluscardenabbey.org Email: www.pluscardenabbey.org

Queen's Cross Church, Glasgow

[131 (H4)] Off M8, 0.5 miles W of centre, 870 Garscube Road. (NGR: NS 575655 LR: 64)

The outstanding church, now the headquarters for the Charles Rennie Mackintosh Society, is the only one designed by Mackintosh. It was built in 1898, but has been extensively restored. There is a small exhibition area, reference library and specialist shop.

Guided tours by appt. Explanatory displays. Gift shop. Refreshments. WC. Car and some coach parking. Donations.

Open all year, Mon-Sat 10.00-17.00, Sun 14.00-17.00; closed some pub hols.

Tel: 0141 946 6600   Fax: 0141 945 2321

Web: www.crmsociety.com   Email: info@crmsociety.com

Restenneth Priory (HS)

[132 (F6)] Off B9113, 1.5 miles NE of Forfar. (NGR: NO 482516 LR: 54)

This is said to be where St Curitan or Boniface baptised Nechtan, King of Picts, and Nechtan is said to have founded a monastery here in 710: this conversion seems somewhat late, though. The priory, dedicated to St Peter, was established in the 12th century by Malcolm IV, and was built on the site of the earlier church. The church was used by the parish until 1590, and then as a burial place for the Dempster and Hunter families. It once stood on an island in a loch, but this was drained in the 19th century. The chancel of the church and tower (the base of which may date from the 8th century) survive, but the other buildings and cloister are more ruinous. There are several medieval cross-slabs, and a gold and sapphire ring, found at the priory, is now on display at the Meffan in Forfar .

Parking.

Access at all reasonable times.

Rona

[133 (A3)] 44 miles NE of Butt of Lewis, Rona. (NGR: HW 809323 LR: 8)

There was a cell or hermitage here, established by St Ronan (a whale helped him reach here) in the 7th or 8th century, and there is a small oratory – this is one of the most complete groups of buildings from the early church in Scotland. There are several cross-incised burial markers, dating from the 7th to 12th centuries. The island is accessible from Ness (in calm weather). It is a National Nature Reserve, in the care of Scottish National Heritage, from whom permission should be sought before visiting. There are many seabirds and a seal colony.

Boats can be hired from Lewis but require booking well in advance. Visitors are strongly advised to contact Scottish Natural Heritage before considering a trip as it is extremely difficult to reach.

Tel: 01851 705258

Rosslyn Chapel

[134 (H5)] Off A701, 6 miles S of Edinburgh, Midlothian. (NGR: NT 275630 LR: 66)

Situated above wooded Roslin Glen and overlooking the River Esk, Rosslyn Chapel, founded by William Sinclair, Earl of Caithness and Orkney, in 1446 is one of the most fascinating churches in Scotland. It was never completed, (although the part that was finished is magnificent): only the choir and parts of the transepts were built. The roof is vaulted in stone and there are a mass of flying buttresses to carry the weight. The chapel is richly carved with Biblical stories, and has the largest number of Green Men found in any medieval building, as well as the famous ornately carved Apprentice Pillar. It was dedicated to St Matthew and intended as a collegiate establishment. The crypt is especially dark and atmospheric, and in the burial vault are ten of the Earls of Roslin and their kin, said to be laid out in their armour without coffins. Roslin Castle is nearby, and there are picturesque walks through the glen.

Guided tours available. Explanatory displays. Gift shop. Tearoom. WC.
Disabled access. Car and coach parking. Group concessions. £.
Open all year, Mon-Sat 10.00-17.00, Sun 12.00-16.45.
Tel: 0131 440 2159   Web: www.rosslyn-chapel.com   Email: rosslynch@aol.com

Ruthwell Cross (HS)

[135 (I5)] Off B724, 9 miles SE of Dumfries, Ruthwell. (NGR: NY 100682   LR: 85)
A magnificent Anglian carved cross, some 17 feet high and dating from the 7th century, decorated with biblical scenes, foliage and beasts. The General Assembly decided it should be smashed and buried in 1640, but it was later pieced together from the broken remains: there is information about the reconstruction in the Savings Banks Museum in Ruthwell.
Parking.
Access can be arranged by contacting the keyholder (tel: 01387 870429).

Saddell Abbey

[136 (H3)] On B842, 6 miles N of Campbeltown, Argyll. (NGR: NR 785321   LR: 68)
The abbey founded as a Cistercian establishment, dedicated to the Blessed Virgin Mary, by Somerled of the Isles (or Reginald his son) around 1160: Somerled is said to be buried here. Much of the stone was used to build nearby Saddell Castle and little now remains, although the ruins are in a pleasant wooded location. There are very impressive medieval grave slabs, carved in high relief, and a reconstructed 15th-century cross, all protected in a modern building.
Information boards. Parking.
Access at all reasonable times.

Seton Collegiate Church (HS)

[137 (H6)] On A198, 5.5 miles W of Haddington, East Lothian. (NGR: NT 418751   LR: 66)
The collegiate church, dedicated to St Mary and the Holy Cross, was founded in 1492 on an older site by the 4th Lord Seton (who was killed at Flodden in 1513). The roof of the church is vaulted, and transepts were added in the 16th century, as was a square rib-vaulted tower, although the choir is gone. The church was

sacked by the English in 1544, and later used as a farm building. It was restored in 1878, and there are several fine stone tombs within the church.
Explanatory displays. Sales area. Car and coach parking. £.
Open Apr-Sep, daily 9.00-18.30, last ticket 18.00.
Tel: 01875 813334

Shandwick Cross-Slab

[138 (D5)] Off B9166, 4 miles SE of Tain, S of Balintore, Shandwick, Ross and Cromarty. (NGR: NH 855747 LR: 21)
Set in a panoramic location overlooking the sea, this is a very impressive Pictish cross-

Seton Collegiate Church (see previous page)

slab, nine foot high and enclosed in a glass box for protection. One side has a cross of protruding bosses, as well as angels, beasts and interlaced snakes; the other is divided into five panels with Pictish symbols, groups of animals, men and riders, and a fine panel of interlacing spirals. The stone may have been moved from its original position after being blown over in a storm. The recreated Hilton of Cadboll stone is nearby.
Parking nearby with care.
Access at all reasonable times: over stile, view from exterior of glass box.
Tel: 01862 832525 (Shandwick Stone Trust)

Soutra Aisle

[139 (H6)] On B6368, 8 miles SE of Gorebridge, Lothian. (NGR: NT 453583 LR: 66)
Commanding excellent, if sometimes windswept, views, there was a hospital here, founded by Malcolm IV around 1164, and dedicated to the Holy Trinity. It was for use by travellers, pilgrims and poor people, and had an infirmary. The church continued to be used by the parish until 1618 after the hospital was abandoned, but all that now remains is one vaulted aisle, used as a burial place by the Pringles of Soutra. Nearby was the Trinity Well [NT 452588], famous for the healing power of the waters, but this has gone. The Roman road Dere Street runs nearby, and there is now a wind farm.
Open all year: tel 01875 833248 10.00-12.00 to arrange tours or lectures.

St Andrews Cathedral (HS)

[140 (G6)] Off A91, St Andrews, Fife. (NGR: NO 516166 LR: 59)

This was the largest and one of the most impressive churches in Scotland, and remains an outstanding ruin dominating the fascinating city of St Andrews.

St Regulus, or Rule, is said to have founded a monastery here in the 5th, 6th or 7th century and brought a relic or relics of St Andrew from Greece. Alternatively they were brought here in 733 by Acca, Bishop of Hexham. The Bishopric was transferred from Abernethy in 908. The adjoining Augustinian priory was founded in 1144 by Robert, Bishop of St Andrews. The church of the time – the tower of which, St Rule's Tower, and part of the choir survives and dates from as early as 1070 – was too small, so a large new cathedral was begun. The cruciform building, with aisled

nave and choir and a central tower, was consecrated in 1318, but had to be rebuilt after a fire in 1380. St Andrews was a major pilgrimage site in medieval times, and there is a well in the floor of the cathedral. After the Reformation, the buildings fell into disuse and much was demolished.

The museum, in the former cloister, houses a large and magnificent collection of Christian and early medieval sculpture, including cross-slabs, effigies, and other carving, and featuring the splendid St Andrews Sarcophagus, which is decorated with scenes from the life of David, carved in high relief.

St Rule's Tower is also open to the public, and there are magnificent views from the top. The impressive precinct wall of the cathedral also survives, and there are foundations of St Mary on the Rock, possibly founded in the 9th century but demolished in 1559, near the harbour.

The castle, which was used by the bishops and archbishops, is nearby: Cardinal David Beaton was killed there and then hung naked from the walls. In St Andrews, there are many other museums and attractions, including St Salvator's College Chapel in North Street and the ruinous north transept of Blackfriars, a Dominican establishment, in South Street.

Cathedral: Visitor centre. Explanatory boards. Gift shop. Car parking nearby.
Group concessions. £. Combined ticket cathedral/castle available (££).
[Museum and St Rule's Tower] Open all year: Apr-Sep, daily 9.30-18.30; Oct-Mar, daily 9.30-16.30; last ticket sold 30 mins before closing; closed 25/26 Dec and 1/2 Jan; cathedral ruins open all year.
Tel: 01334 472563

St Andrews Cathedral, Inverness

[141 (D4)] Off A82, Ardross Street, W bank of River Ness, Inverness, Highlands.
(NGR: NH 665449 LR: 26)
Standing by the River Ness, the Gothic twin-towered cathedral was built in 1886-9, and has an octagonal chapter house, pillars of granite, stained glass, sculpture and a fine font.

Explanatory displays. Gift shop. Tearoom. WC. Parking nearby.
Cathedral open daily, 8.30-18.00 (later in summer);
tearoom open May-Sep, 10.30-15.30.
Tel: 01463 233535

St Athernase Church, Leuchars

[142 (G6)] Off A919, Leuchars, Fife. (NGR: NO 455215 LR: 59)
One of the finest Romanesque churches in Scotland, the chancel and apse, with

blind arcades, survive from a 12th-century church, dedicated to St Athernase, although little is known about him. It was granted to the canons of St Andrews by Nes, Lord of Lochore, in 1185. The belfry was added about 1700, and the nave restored in 1858.
Sales area. WC. Parking nearby.
Open Mar-Oct, daily 9.30-18.00.
Tel: 01334 838884

St Blane's Church, Kingarth (HS)

[143 (H4)] Off A844, 2 miles S of Kingarth, Bute. (NGR: NS 094535 LR: 63)

In a fabulous tranquil location with fine views is the site of a 6th-century monastery, associated with St Catan and St Blane, who was born on Bute. The site is enclosed by a wall, and there are several ruinous buildings, including The Cauldron, recorded as a place of punishment, and the ruinous 12th-century chapel,

with a finely decorated chancel arch. There is also an upper and lower burial ground with some fine markers, the upper yard being used for men, while the lower was for women. A nearby spring, a reputed holy and wishing well, is called St Blane's Well.

Parking.

Access at all reasonable times – short walk to site: may be muddy.

St Bride's Church, Douglas (HS)

[144 (H5)] Off A70, 9 miles S of Lanark, Main Street, Douglas. (NGR: NS 835309 LR: 72)

Although there was an earlier church here, the present remnant dates from 1330 and later, consisting of the reroofed chancel and the remains of the south transept. There is the stone effigy of Good Sir James Douglas, who died in 1331 taking Robert the Bruce's heart on pilgrimage. Other memorials include that of Archibald Douglas, 5th Earl of Douglas, who died in 1438; James, 7th Earl, who died in 1443; and his wife Beatrice Sinclair.

Parking nearby.

Access at all reasonable times – instruction for key on notice on gate.

Tel: 01555 851657/0131 668 8800

St Bridget's Kirk, Dalgety (HS)

[145 (H5)] Off A921, 5 miles SE of Dunfermline, Dalgety, Fife. (NGR: NT 169838 LR: 66)
Overlooking the Forth are the ruins of a long church, dedicated to St Bridget, possibly dating from the 12th century, but altered in the 17th century. There is a burial vault at one end with a laird's loft above, and Alexander Seton, Earl of Dunfermline and Chancellor of Scotland, who died in 1622, is buried here. There are some interesting markers in the burial ground. Nothing survives of Dalgety House, Seton's favourite residence, and there was a village of Dalgety, about 0.5 miles south-east of the church, but again there are no remains.
Parking nearby.
Church: access at all reasonable times.

St Clement's Church, Rodel (HS)

[146 (D2)] On A859, 2.5 miles SE of Leverburgh, S of Harris. (NGR: NG 047833 LR: 18)
The fine 16th-century cruciform church, has a strong square tower at one end, which may date from the 13th-century. It was dedicated to St Clement, a Bishop

of Dunblane in the 13th century. The splendid carved tomb of Alasdair Crotach MacLeod, built in 1528, reads: 'this tomb was prepared by Lord Alexander, son of Willielmus MacLeod, Lord of Dunvegan, in the year of Our Lord 1528'. There is another tomb, with a stone effigy of 1539. There are several carved slabs, and a disc-headed cross, as well as a Sheila na Gig on the outside of the south wall of the tower, which is an interesting adornment for the outside of a church.
Parking nearby.
Access at all reasonable times.

St Columba's Cave

[147 (H3)] Off B8024, 12 miles SW of Lochgilphead, 1 mile N of Ellary, Knapdale, Argyll. (NGR: NR 751768   LR: 62)

In a scenic setting by the shore of Loch Caolisport, the cave is associated with St Columba's arrival in Scotland from Ireland, and has a rock-cut shelf with an altar, above which crosses have been carved in the wall. A basin may have been used as a font. A ruined chapel, dating from the 13th century, stands nearby, and there is another cave: these caves were both used in Prehistoric times.

Parking nearby.

Access at all reasonable times.

St Columba's Church (Ui), Aignish

[148 (C2)] Off A866, 3.5 miles E of Stornoway, Aignish, Lewis. (NGR: NB 484322   LR: 8)

St Catan is said to have had a monastery here in the 6th or 7th centuries, although the ruinous rectangular church probably dates from the 14th century. It was used as a burial place by the MacLeods of Lewis. In the church there are the carved tombs and stones effigies of Roderick, 7th chief; and Margaret, daughter of Roderick MacLeod of Lewis, who died in 1503. There is an interesting burial ground.

Car parking.

Access at all reasonable times.

St Conan's Kirk, Lochawe

[149 (G4)] On A85, 4 miles E of Dalmally, 0.5 miles W of Lochawe, Argyll. (NGR: NN 116268   LR: 50)

St Conan is said to have lived in Glenorchy, and is the patron saint of Lorne. The modern church is a fabulous airy building in different architectural styles, with a cloister garth and semi-circular apse and ambulatory. There is the Bruce Chapel, which has a fragment of bone reputed to be from Robert the Bruce, and an effigy of the Campbell builder.

Parking.

Open at all reasonable times.

St Congan's Church, Turriff

[150 (D6)] Off B9025, Turriff, Aberdeenshire. (NGR: NJ 722498   LR: 29)

St Congan had a monastery here, but the long and ruinous church dates from the 13th century and has a belfry of 1635 (with a bell dated 1556) and a working clock. There are also several splendid carved burial markers, dating from the 16th and 17th centuries, including the fabulous monument of the Barclays of Tolly, and fragments of other carved stones.

Access at all reasonable times.

St Duthac's Chapel, Tain

[151 (D5)] On B9174, Tain, near the sea, Ross-shire. (NGR: NH 786823 LR: 21)

This is said to be the birthplace of St Duthac and was a place of pilgrimage. The ruins of the rectangular chapel date from the 13th century. It was from near the church that Elizabeth, Queen of Scots and wife of Robert the Bruce, and other of his womenfolk, were captured by the Earl of Ross in 1306. Despite being an area of sanctuary, they were delivered into the hands of Edward I of England. The church was torched in 1429 when MacNeil of Creich burned Mowat of Freswick and his men during a feud.

Parking nearby.

Access at all reasonable times.

St Duthac's Church, Tain

[152 (D5)] On B9174, High Street, Tain, Ross-shire. (NGR: NH 780821 LR: 21)

Tain was a place of pilgrimage, and thousands of pilgrims visited the shrine of St Duthac, including James IV and James V, who walked here barefoot. The church became a collegiate establishment in 1487, founded by Thomas Hay, Bishop of Ross, and is a fine building, dating from the 14th and 15th centuries. It has large windows with restored tracery, and a statue on the outside of the west wall is thought to be that of St Duthac, which unusually survived the Reformation. Around 1815, the church fell into disrepair, although it was restored and re-roofed in 1877.

There is a nearby visitor centre, Tain Through Time, which has displays and an audiovisual interpretation of the history of Tain as a centre of pilgrimage.

Visitor centre (£).

Parking nearby.

Open all year.

St Fillan's Cave, Pittenweem

[153 (G6)] Off A917, 1 mile W of Anstruther, Cove Wynd, Pittenweem, Fife.
(NGR: NO 550024 LR: 59)

The cave is associated with St Fillan, who was a hermit here for many years, and was renovated in 1935 and rededicated for worship.

Car parking. £

Open all year: Easter-Oct, Mon-Sat 9.00-17.30; Nov-Easter, Tue-Sat 9.00-17.30, Sun 12.00-17.00. Key from The Gingerbread Horse, 9 High Street, Pittenweem.
Tel: 01333 311495 Fax: 01333 312212

St Fillan's Church, Aberdour

[154 (H5)] Off A921, 6.5 miles SW of Kirkcaldy, Hawkcraig Road, Aberdour, Fife.
(NGR: NT 194856 LR: 66)

Standing in the picturesque village above the harbour, the church, which is dedicated to St Fillan, dates from the 12th century or earlier. It was enlarged with an aisle in the 15th century, then again in the 17th century. The church deteriorated from the 18th century, but was restored in 1925. There is an interesting burial ground. It is near to Aberdour Castle (which is also open to the public (HS)) and is a fine building with grand gardens.

Parking nearby.

Open all year.

St Giles Cathedral, Edinburgh

[155 (H5)] Off A1, High Street (Royal Mile). (NGR: NT 257735 LR: 66)

Although there has been a church here since 854 or earlier, the present building dates substantially from the 14th and 15th centuries, after the church had been sacked by the English in 1385. It was dedicated to St Giles, made a collegiate establishment in 1466 by James III, and has an impressive crown steeple, which was added in 1495. John Knox was minister and preached here in the 16th century, and it was here that Jenny Geddes flung her stool in outrage at the introduction of a new prayer book in 1637. St Giles was the post-Reformation bishop's seat from 1633-9 and then 1662-90, hence it is called a cathedral. There are several aisles which house separate chapels and numerous memorials, including to the Marquis of Montrose and Earl of Argyll, Robert Louis Stevenson and Robert Burns. There is also fine stained glass, a magnificent organ, and the Thistle Chapel, designed by Sir Robert Lorimer.

Explanatory displays. Guides on duty at all times. Gift shop. Restaurant. WC. Limited disabled access. Parking nearby (but often difficult).

Open all year: Easter-mid Sep, Mon-Fri 9.00-19.00, Sat 9.00-17.00, Sun 13.00-17.00; mid-Sep-Easter, Mon-Sat 9.00-17.00, Sun 13.00-17.00.
Tel: 0131 225 9442 Fax: 0131 225 9576 Web: www.stgiles.net Email: stgiles@hotmail.com

St John the Baptist's Church, Ayr

[156 (I4)] Off A719, Ayr, Ayrshire. (NGR: NS 334220 LR: 70)

The once splendid former parish church of Ayr, dedicated to St John the Baptist and dating from 1233, was cruciform in plan and some 140 feet long. Only the strong tall tower remains, with a corbelled-out parapet, while all else has gone. Robert the Bruce held a parliament here in 1315, the church and burial ground were enclosed by a fort (sections of which survive) built by Cromwell in the 1650s, but most of the church was demolished in the 18th century.

Open to the public by arrangement - tel: 01292 286385; other times view from exterior.

St John's Church, Edinburgh

[157 (H5)] W end of Princes Street, Edinburgh. (NGR: NT 248736 LR: 66)

The tall aisled church, designed by William Burn, dates from the early 19th century, and has a fine collection of stained glass, as well as modern paintings and sculpture. In the burial ground are many famous Scots, including Sir Henry Raeburn, the famous portrait painter, and James Donaldson, founder of Donaldson's School for the Deaf.

Guided tours by arrangement. Gift shop. Cafe. WC. Disabled access.

Open all year, daily from 7.30.

Tel: 0131 229 7565 Fax: 0131 229 2561 Email: saintjohnsoffice@btconnect.com

St John's Church, Gamrie

[158 (D6)] Off B9031, 6 miles E of Banff, W of Gardenstown, Banff and Buchan.
(NGR: NJ 791644 LR: 30)

In a wonderful position with great views over Gamrie Bay, the ruinous rectangular church dates from the 16th century, but was founded in 1004. It was dedicated to St John the Evangelist, and formerly known as the Kirk of Skulls. Three skulls were displayed east of the pulpit, the heads of Norsemen defeated at the Battle of Bloody Pots in 1004. One of the skulls is now in Banff Museum. There is a good burial ground with monuments from the 17th century.

Access at all reasonable times: care should be taken.

St John's Kirk, Perth

[159 (G5)] Off A912, St John Street, centre of Perth. (NGR: NO 121233 LR: 58)

There was a church here from early times, and parts of the present impressive building may date from the 12th century. It was consecrated in 1242 and dedicated to St John the Baptist (Perth is also known as St John's Town of Perth, hence the name of the local football team), then largely rebuilt in the 15th century, and restored in the 1920s-30s. The kirk is cruciform in plan with a large central tower and tall spire, aisles and transepts. The church has the original roof of the choir, fine modern stained glass, a statue of John the Baptist, and carving from the life of Christ on the barrel vaulting of the nave. There is also a good collection of bells, some dating from before the Reformation.

The heart of Alexander III and the body of James I are said to be buried here. In 1559 John Knox preached against idolatry, and his congregation 'purged' the church, which had some 40 altars, then ransacked the houses of the Blackfriars, Greyfriars and Charterhouse monks, as well as the abbeys of Coupar Angus and Scone. Charles I, Cromwell, Charles II and Bonnie Prince Charlie all visited.

Guided tours by arrangement. Disabled access. Induction loop. Parking nearby.

Open Easter-Sep, Mon-Sat 10.00-16.00, Sun 12.00-14.00; Oct-Apr tel to confirm.

Tel: 01738 626520

St Machar's Cathedral, Old Aberdeen

[160 (E7)] Off A956, The Chanonry, N of Aberdeen. (NGR: NJ 939088 LR: 38)

There was a monastery here from 580 (or earlier), founded by St Machar, patron saint of Aberdeen, and a cathedral was established in 1140. The present building dates mostly from 1350-1520, and the aisled nave and impressive west front with solid twin towers and short spires survive as the parish church, while the transepts are ruinous (the central tower collapsed in 1688). The chancel, left to deteriorate after the Reformation, is largely gone. There is an impressive heraldic ceiling of panelled oak dating from 1520, which is decorated with the coats of arms of many noble families; and impressive stained-glass windows. A collection of medieval charters is housed in the Charter Room. There are also the tombs of Bishop Gavin Dunbar, who died in 1532 and commissioned the ceiling, and Bishop

Lichton, who had the west front built between 1422-40. There is an interesting burial ground with good memorials.

Guided tours by appt. Gift shop. WC. Disabled access and induction loop. Parking.

Open all year, daily 9.00-17.00 (except for weddings, funerals and unscheduled special events).

Tel: 01224 485988

St Magnus Cathedral, Kirkwall

[161 (A6)] Town centre, Broad Street, Kirkwall, Orkney. (NGR: HY 449112 LR: 6)

The magnificent cathedral is one of the finest churches in Scotland. It dates substantially from 1137-1200 and was completed about 1500. The cathedral is dedicated to St Magnus the Martyr, grandson to Thorfinn the Mighty, whose bones are interred within the church in the massive east choir pillar. The church was founded by Earl Rognvald Kolson in the 12th century, whose remains are also here. He brought Magnus's bones from Birsay, including the skull showing the blow of the axe that had killed him. The cathedral survived the Reformation intact and is used at the parish church. The cathedral is cruciform in plan, the nave and choir have aisles, and there is a tall central

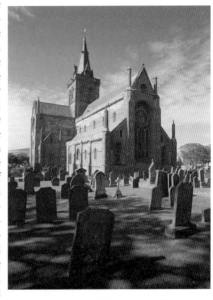

tower with a spire: the west front is particularly good. There are excellent stained-glass windows, an interesting burial ground, and the St Magnus Centre has a 15-minute video.

Explanatory displays. Disabled access to half of the building. Parking nearby.

Open Apr-Sep, Mon-Sat 9.00-18.00, Sun 14.00-18.00; Oct-Mar, Mon-Sat 9.00-13.00 and 14.00-17.00.

Tel: 01856 874894 Fax: 01856 875846

Web: www.orkneyheritage.com Email: steve.callaghan@orkney.gov.uk

St Magnus Church, Birsay

[162 (A5)] On A966, 12 miles N of Stromness, Birsay, Orkney. (NGR: HY 248276 LR: 6)
The long low church, dating from 1064, was rebuilt in 1664 and 1760, restored in 1986, and replaced the cruciform Christ's Kirk which dated from 1050 and may have been used by the bishops of Orkney. St Magnus's body was brought here after from Egilsay after he was slain, and many miracles were then attributed to his remains. His bones were later taken to St Magnus Cathedral in Kirkwall, where they still rest in one of the pillars. The Earl's Palace at Birsay is across the road from the church, and the Brough of Birsay is nearby.
WC nearby. Parking nearby.
Open Apr-Sep, daily: key available all year from the village shop.

St Magnus Church, Egilsay (HS)

[163 (A6)] W side of Egilsay, E of Rousay, Orkney. (NGR: HY 467303 LR: 6)
The peaceful island is where Earl Magnus prayed before his murder and martyrdom in 1117. The solid ruinous church, dating from the 12th century, consists of a nave, square-ended vaulted chancel, and round Irish-style tower, lowered but formerly with a beehive-type roof. The present church may have been built to commemorate the martyrdom, although it may predate it.
Access at all reasonable times.
Tel: 01856 841815

St Margaret's Cave, Dunfermline

[164 (H5)] Off A994, Bruce Street car park, Dunfermline. (NGR: NT 087873 LR: 65)
The cave is associated with St Margaret, and was a place of pilgrimage in medieval times. Dunfermline Abbey is nearby (see separate entry).
Explanatory displays. Gift shop. Car and coach parking.
Open Easter-Sep, daily 11.00-16.00.
Tel: 01383 314228/313838

St Margaret's Chapel, Edinburgh Castle (HS)

[165 (H5)] Off A1, in the centre of Edinburgh. (NGR: NT 252735 LR: 66)
Standing on a high rock, Edinburgh Castle was one of the strongest and most important fortresses in Scotland. The oldest building in the complex is a small Romanesque chapel of the early 12th century, dedicated to St Margaret, and believed to have been built by David I. The fine Romanesque chancel arch survives, and a copy of St Margaret's gospel book can be seen here. St Margaret had died at the castle in 1093 after learning of her husband's death at Alnwick and was buried with her husband at Dunfermline. The castle has many attractions, and is the home of the Scottish crown jewels, the great cannon Mons Meg, and

the Stone of Destiny; and has spectacular views over the capital.

Edinburgh Castle: Explanatory displays. Audio-guide tour. Guided tours. Gift shop. Restaurant. WC. Disabled access. Visitors with a disability can be taken to the top of the castle by a courtesy vehicle; ramps and lift access to Crown Jewels and Stone of Destiny. Parking (except during Tattoo). £££.

Open all year: Apr-Sep, daily 9.30-17.15 (last ticket sold); Oct-Mar, daily 9.30-16.15 (last ticket sold), castle closes 45 mins after last ticket is sold; times may be altered during Tattoo and state occasions; closed 25/26 Dec and 1/2 Jan.

Tel: 0131 225 9846

St Mary's Cathedral, Glasgow

[166 (H4)] Off A82 from M8, 300 Great Western Road. (NGR: NS 578669   LR: 64)

The fine Gothic church was designed by Sir George Gilbert Scott, and there are contemporary murals by Gwyneth Leech.

Bookshop. Partial disabled access. Limited parking.

Open all year, daily Mon-Fri 9.30-17.45, Sat 9.30-12.00; tel for services; bookshop Mon-Fri, 10.00-16.00.

Tel: 0141 339 6691   Fax: 0141 339 6691

St Mary's Chapel, Crosskirk (HS)

[167 (B5)] Off A836, 6 miles NW of Thurso, Caithness. (NGR: ND 024700   LR: 12)

The simple dry-stone chapel, dedicated to St Mary, has a rectangular chancel and square nave. It probably dates from the 12th century, is roofless but the walls are complete. The building probably had a thatched roof, and stands in a walled burial ground. Part of it was used as a burial place by the Gunn family in the 19th century, and to the south is a healing well, which was also dedicated to St Mary.

Parking nearby.

Access at all reasonable times – walk to chapel (0.75 miles) may be muddy.

Tel: 01667 460232

St Mary's Church, Grandtully (HS)

[168 (G5)] Off A827, 3 miles NE of Aberfeldy, Perthshire. (NGR: NN 886505   LR: 52)

Standing in an old burial ground, the long low whitewashed church dates from 1533 and is a remarkable survivor from before the Reformation. It was remodelled in 1633, when a fine extravagantly painted ceiling was installed, illustrating heraldic, biblical and symbolic subjects, and commissioned by Sir William Stewart and Agnes Moncrieffe. This is contemporary with the Skelmorlie Aisle of Largs Old Kirk (see separate entry).

Parking.

Access at all reasonable times.

St Mary's Church, Haddington

[169 (H6)] Off A6093, Sidegate, Haddington, East Lothian. (NGR: NT 518736 LR: 66)

In the picturesque town by the River Tyne, the church is a large cruciform build-ing, dedicated to St Mary, with an aisled nave and choir, central tower and tran-septs. The roof is vaulted, apart from the restored nave. There are interesting medieval carvings, including Green Men and a scallop shell, the latter the sign of

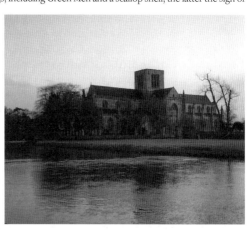

a place of pil-grimage. The church houses a marble monu-ment to John Maitland, Lord Thirlestane and Chancellor of Scotland, who died in 1595, his wife and son, now known as 'The Chapel of the Three Kings'. Beneath is the Lauder-dale family vault. The church stands in a burial ground. The foundations of St Martin's Kirk [NT 521739], a formerly splendid church dating from the 12th cen-tury, are also located in Haddington.

Guided tours available. Explanatory displays. Printed guides in several languages. Gift and book shop. Tearoom. WC. Picnic area by river. Children's activity area. Brass rubbing by arrangement. Disabled access. Car and coach access.

Open Apr-Sep, Mon-Sat 11.00-16.00, Sun 14.00-16.30.

Tel: 01620 823109 Web: www.kylemore.btinternet.co.uk/stmarys.htm
Email: chrystals@btinternet.com

St Mary's Church, Monymusk

[170 (E6)] Off B993, 6.5 miles SW of Inverurie, Aberdeenshire. (NGR: NJ 684152 LR: 38)

Standing on the site of an early monastery of Culdees in the quiet village, the nave, chancel arch and parts of the large west tower (which was formerly taller) date from 1170, when a priory of Augustinian canons was founded here, dedi-cated to St Mary the Virgin. The priory was burnt in 1544, and its lands seized by the Forbeses of Corsindae, who built the nearby castle [NJ 688155]. The church was greatly altered in later centuries, most of the choir being used as the burial place for the Grant family, but it was restored in 1929 and is an interesting building. There are fine stained-glass windows.

The Monymusk Stone, a Pictish carved stone, is housed in the church along with other stones dating from the 7th-9th centuries. The Monymusk Reliquary, which once held the relics of St Columba, was also sometimes displayed here, but is now kept in the Museum of Scotland in Edinburgh (see separate entry).
Parking nearby. Disabled access on request.
Open Apr-Oct, daylight hours; Sun all year for worship; other times by arrangement: tel 01467 651470 or contact euanglen@aol.com

St Mary's Church, Rothesay (HS)

[171 (H4)] On A845, 0.5 miles S of Rothesay Castle, Bute. (NGR: NS 086637 LR: 63)
Standing by the modern parish church, the small rectangular chapel, dedicated to St Mary and dating from the 13th century, is all that remains of Ladykirk. The old church was also dedicated to St Brioc, and used as the cathedral of the Isles. The reroofed chapel, houses two stone effigies: one a warrior, probably a Stewart of Menteith. The burial ground has many outstanding 19th-century markers and monuments. A spring, housed in a small building, is called St Mary's Well.
Parking nearby.
Open Apr-Sep, daily 8.00-17.00; Oct-Mar, Sat-Thu 8.00-17.00.

St Mary's Episcopal Cathedral, Edinburgh

[172 (H5)] 0.5 miles W of city centre, Palmerston Place. (NGR: NT 241735 LR: 66)
The large Gothic cathedral, dedicated to St Mary, dates from 1879, while the western towers were added in 1917. The central spire is 276 feet high, and the church has a fine interior. The cathedral has an internationally renowned choir, and in the Song School are restored murals by Phoebe Traquair.
Explanatory displays. Gift stall. Creche. WC. Disabled access, WCs and induction loop. Parking nearby.
Cathedral: open all year, Mon-Fri 7.30-18.00, Sat-Sun 7.30-17.00; Song School: open by appt.
Tel: 0131 225 6293 Fax: 0131 225 3181 Web: www.cathedral.net Email: office@cathedral.net

St Mary's Kirk, Auchindour (HS)

[173 (E6)] Off A97, 8 miles NW of Alford, near Lumsden. (NGR: NJ 477244 LR: 37)
The picturesque ruinous church, dedicated to St Mary, dates from the 13th century, and has a fine Romanesque doorway and 14th-century sacrament house. There are good memorials, and nearby is St Mary's Well, which was used to alleviate toothache.
Parking nearby.
Access to church at all reasonable times: keys available locally.
Tel: 01667 460232

St Mary's Parish Church, Whitekirk

[174 (H6)] On A198, 3.5 miles SE of North Berwick, Whitekirk, East Lothian.
(NGR: NT 596815 LR: 67)

Whitekirk became a place of pilgrimage around 1295 after Agnes, Countess of Dunbar, was healed at a nearby well [NT 598817?]. The number of miracles was

so great that a shrine was built in 1309 and dedicated to St Mary. Around the beginning of the 15th century, James I had pilgrims' hostels built: there were some 15,000 pilgrims in 1413. Whitekirk was visited by Aeneas Sylvius Piccolomini (later Pope Pious II) in 1435 who, after being saved from a storm, walked barefoot to Whitekirk from Dunbar, and suffered from rheumatism for the rest of his life. A fresco in the chapter house of Siena Cathedral records his visit. James IV also visited. This well dried up around 1830, and its location is not certain.

Located in the quiet hamlet of Whitekirk, the present attractive church is largely 15th century, although parts date from the 12th century. It was restored in 1885, burned by suffragettes in 1914, then restored again, and is cruciform in plan with a sturdy central tower. The burial ground has some good markers.

Sales area. WC. Parking nearby.

Open all at all reasonable times.
Tel: 01620 880378

St Michael's Parish Church, Linlithgow

[175 (H5)] Off M9, Kirkgate, Linlithgow. (NGR: NT 003773 LR: 65)

This is one of the finest parish churches in Scotland, and was dedicated in 1242 to St Michael, on the site of an earlier church. The present large aisled church, cruciform in plan, dates mostly from the 15th century, and has a tower at the west end, now with an unusual steeple, added in 1964, to replace a stone crown such as that of St Giles in Edinburgh. There is excellent carving on the west front and a statue of St Michael on the south-west buttress. The church has associations with the Stewart monarchs, particularly James IV (who was warned not to invade England here by a blue-robed apparition) and James V. There are interesting 15th-century relief slabs in the vestry, and some noteworthy memorials in the burial ground. Nearby [NT 004771] is St Michael's Well, which is housed in a stone building, and has a rough carved stone depicting the saint and the words: 'St Michael is Kinde to Strangers'. The magnificent but ruinous Linlithgow Palace, which is associated with many Scottish monarchs, is near the church, and there is a museum, the Linlithgow Story, in the town.

Guided tours by arrangement. Explanatory displays. Gift shop. Picnic area. Parking.
Open May-Sep, daily 10.00-16.30; Oct-Apr, Mon-Fri 10.00-15.00.
Tel: 01506 842188   Web: www.stmichaels-parish.org.uk
Email: stmichael@connectfree.co.uk

St Moluag's Church, Eoropie

[176 (B2)] Off B8014 or B8013, 26 miles N of Stornoway, Lewis. (NGR: NB 519652 LR: 8)
Although there was probably a monastery here in the 6th century, the present rectangular church, dedicated to St Moluag, dates from the 12th century. The church has round arched windows and door, and an adjoining chapel (possibly for use by lepers) only has a squint or viewing hole into the body of the church. The building was restored in 1912, but has no electricity or gas, and is lit by candles and lamps. The church was associated with 'hallow-tide sacrifices' to the sea-god Shony as late as the 17th century, described as a pagan fertility rite.

Parking nearby.
Open Easter-Sep during daylight hours: short walk to church - path may be muddy.

St Monans Parish Church

[177 (G6)] Off A917, 2.5 miles W of Anstruther, Fife. (NGR: NO 523014 LR: 59)

St Monan was slain by Norsemen here in about 870, and the church became a place of pilgrimage, and held his relics. A Dominican friary was founded here in 1477, but this was absorbed into the one at St Andrews, and the church was torched by the English in 1544. It was restored in 1828, and again in 1961.

The large church is situated on an impressive cliff-top location, and dates from 1370. It is T- plan with a rib-vaulted chancel and central tower with a short spire: there is no nave. The church has a 14th-century sedilia, piscina and aumbry, as well as medieval crosses. The burial ground has many interesting memorials
Welcomers on duty. Leaflet. Parking.
Open Apr-Oct.

St Nicholas Buccleuch Parish Church, Dalkeith

[178 (H5)] Off A68/A6094 junction, 6.5 miles SE of Edinburgh, High Street, Midlothian. (NGR: NT 330670 LR: 66)

The parish church became a collegiate establishment in 1406, founded by Sir James Douglas, and it was dedicated to St Nicholas. It was cruciform in plan with a tower at the west end and a choir and polygonal apse, although the choir was abandoned in 1590 and is now ruinous. The nave and transepts date from 1854, and the inside has been greatly altered.

James Douglas, 1st Earl of Morton, and his wife Joanna, daughter of James I, are buried in the choir, their tomb marked by stone effigies, dating from around 1498. There are also some interesting markers in the burial ground, including to the Douglases.
Refreshments. WC. Disabled access. Parking nearby.
Open Easter Sun-end Sep, Mon-Fri 10.00-16.00, Sun 10.00-11.00; or by appt.
Tel: 0131 663 0799   Web: www.btinternet.com~stnicholasbuccleuch
Email: edward.andrews@btinternet.com

St Ninian's Cave, Physgill (HS)

[179 (J4)] Off A747, 4 miles SW of Whithorn, Physgill, Dumfries and Galloway. (NGR: NX 421359 LR: 83)

The cave is said to have been the retreat of St Ninian from Whithorn. Crosses are carved on the walls, probably by pilgrims, and carved stones have also been found during excavations. Eleven stones, dating from the 11th century or earlier, which were found here are now at Whithorn. The cave, although it has partially collapsed, is still a place of pilgrimage.
Car and coach parking nearby.
Access at all times – involves walk from car park.

St Ninian's Chapel, Isle of Whithorn (HS)

[180 (J4)] Off A750, 2 miles SE of Whithorn, Galloway. (NGR: NX 479362 LR: 83)
In a peaceful location by the sea, the small ruined chapel stands on a site associated with St Ninian, and dates from the 13th century. It was used by pilgrims on their way from Ireland and the Isle of Man to St Ninian's shrine at Whithorn.
Car and coach parking nearby.
Access at all reasonable times – involves walk.

St Orland's Stone, Cossans (HS)

[181 (G6)] Off A928, 3.5 miles W of Forfar, Angus. (NGR: NO 401500 LR: 54)
The Pictish cross-slab, called St Orland's Stone, probably marks the site of an early monastery. One side has a full-length ringed cross, filled with interlaced patterns, while the other is framed by two fish-tailed serpents, as at Dunfallandy (see separate entry). There are also Pictish symbols, four horsemen and hounds, a boat, and a beast attacking a bull.
Parking nearby.
Access at all reasonable times.

St Peter's Church, Duffus (HS)

[182 (D5)] Off B9012, Duffus, Moray. (NGR: NJ 175688 LR: 28)
Much of the fine ruin dates from the 18th century, but there is a good 16th-century vaulted porch and the base of a 14th-century tower, now the Sutherland burial vault. In the burial ground is St Peter's Cross, a medieval market cross (markets were regularly held in kirkyards), as well as noteworthy burial markers.
Parking nearby.
Access at all reasonable times.

St Peter's Church, Thurso

[183 (B5)] Off A882, Wilson Lane, Thurso. (NGR: ND 120686   LR: 12)

The church, dating from the 16th century but with earlier work, was dedicated to St Peter, and is now ruinous. It was cruciform in plan, and was altered after the Reformation. There is a small vaulted cell, stair tower and passageway, and a runic inscription on one wall. It stands in a packed burial ground with some good markers.

Open summer; other times key available from the Town Hall.

St Queran's Well, Islesteps

[184 (I5)] Off A710, 2.5 miles SE of Dumfries. (NGR: NX 956722   LR: 84)

The spring is a healing and clootie well, dedicated to St Queran or Kiaran, and believed to have been particularly effective for women and children. When it was excavated in 1870, 100s of coins and pins were found in the spring. The well is still used, and many items of clothing are still left here.

Parking nearby.

Access at all reasonable times: walk to well.

St Serf's Church, Dunning (HS)

[185 (G5)] On B8062 or B934, 5 miles E of Auchterarder, Dunning, Perthshire.
(NGR: NO 019145   LR: 58)

A church was founded here in the 6th century by St Serf after he had slain a dragon by using just his staff, and there was a Culdee community here. The lofty rectangular parish church has a square 75-foot-high Romanesque tower and tower arch, dating to about 1200-10, although the body of the church was rebuilt in 1810. The fine Dupplin Cross (see separate entry) is housed here.

Parking nearby.

Keys available locally.

St Serf's Church, Tullibody

[186 (G5)] On B9140, 5 miles NE of Stirling, Menstrie Road, N of Tullibody, Clackman-nanshire. (NGR: NS 860953   LR: 58)

In an open location are the ruins of a rectangular church, dating from the 16th century and rebuilt after being destroyed in 1559 by forces of Mary of Guise to replace a demolished bridge. There was a church here from 1149, dedicated to St Serf, but it was stripped and unroofed in 1916 after becoming unsafe. This is the site of the mausoleum of the Abercrombies of Tullibody, and there are many interesting memorials in the burial ground, dating from the 18th century, as well as the Maiden Stone, the remains of a stone coffin.

Access at all reasonable times.

St Ternan's Church, Arbuthnott

[187 (F6)] Off B967, 5.5 miles NE of Laurencekirk, SE of Arbuthnott, Kincardine and Deeside. (NGR: NO 801746 LR: 45)

St Ternan was born here, and there was a church here from early times, although the present building dates from 1242. It is a fascinating building in a peaceful location, rectangular in plan with a round bell tower at the west end, dating from

about 1500. The church was gutted by fire in 1889, but was restored. In the Arbuthnott Aisle, formerly the Lady Chapel, is a 13th-century stone effigy of Hugh Arbuthnott. Above the aisle is the Priest's Room, with stone window seats and a squint to the chapel. Lewis Grassic Gibbon is buried in the churchyard, and there are other interesting memorials.

Disabled limited access. Parking nearby.
Open all year.

St Triduana's Chapel, Edinburgh (HS)

[188 (H5)] Restalrig Road South, Restalrig, E of Edinburgh. (NGR: NT 282745 LR: 66)

St Triduana is said to have come to Scotland with either St Curitan or St Rule, and is associated with Rescobie in Angus and Restalrig, where her well was reputed to have healing properties, being especially good for the eyes (after she had skewered her own). St Triduana's Chapel or Well, the lower part of a former two-storey building, is an extremely attractive hexagonal vaulted chamber with a pointed roof, which is reached down a flight of steps. This has been described as

an aisle, well or chapter house, although fresh water still flows from a spring here near one of the outer walls.

The rectangular church, dedicated to St Mary and the Trinity, was raised to a collegiate establishment by James III in the 1460s, and has some interesting details – there is no internal connection from the church to St Triduana's Chapel. The church and chapel were attacked by a reforming mob towards the end of the 16th century, and both buildings remained ruinous until rebuilt and restored in 1836. There are some interesting markers and memorials in the burial ground. *Parking nearby.*

Access can be arranged by contacting St Margaret's Parish Church, Restalrig. Tel: 0131 554 7400/0131 668 8800

St Vigeans Church and Museum, Arbroath

[189 (G6)] Off A933, 0.5 miles N of Arbroath, Angus. (NGR: NO 639429 LR: 54)
Perched on a steep mound in the peaceful hamlet of St Vigeans, the interesting church, surrounded by a burial ground, dates from the 12th century and is dedicated to St Vigean. This was the parish church for Arbroath, and parts may date from 1100, while the tower is 15th century. A museum of early Christian and Pictish sculpture is housed in cottages, including the St Drostan Stone. The crossslab has an Ogham inscription, as well as carvings of beasts, men and symbols. *Parking nearby at Church Hall.*

Church: key available from no 7, over the road from the church; museum: key available locally: check before setting out (0131 668 8800).
Tel: 01241 873206 Email: gaz71@dial.pipex.com

Stobo Kirk

[190 (H5)] Off B712, 4.5 miles SW of Peebles, Stobo, Borders. (NGR: NT 182376 LR: 72)

St Mungo is said to have founded a church here in the 6th century. The kirk, dedicated to him and dating from the 12th century, has a Romanesque nave and narrower chancel. A fine doorway survives within a 16th-century porch, and there is a squat tower at the west end, which was altered in the 16th century, although the base is also probably Norman. The north aisle was restored in 1929. The church houses fine medieval recumbent tombstones, and there are interesting 17th- and 18th-century memorials in the burial ground.

Disabled limited access. Parking nearby.

Open all year.

Tel: 01899 830331 Email: revracheldobie@cs.com

Sueno's Stone, Forres (HS)

[191 (D5)] Off A96, on E edge of Forres, Moray. (NGR: NJ 809653 LR: 27)

A magnificent but weathered carved Pictish stone, dating from the 9th century and more than 22 foot tall. One side has a large ring-headed cross, the shaft of which is filled with interlaced knotwork. The other side is divided into four panels, telling the story of a battle, possibly a victory over the Norsemen.

Parking nearby.

Access at all reasonable times – stone is encased in a glass case for protection – viewing may be difficult in wet weather.

Tel: 01667 460232

Sweetheart Abbey (HS)

[192 (J5)] On A710, 6 miles S of Dumfries, New Abbey, Dumfries and Galloway. (NGR: NX 964663 LR: 84)

The abbey was founded as a Cistercian establishment, dedicated to the Blessed Virgin Mary, in 1273 by Devorgilla of Galloway in memory of her husband, John Balliol – Devorgilla was

Sweetheart Abbey

buried here before the high altar. They were the parents of John, King of Scots, and founded Balliol College, Oxford. Devorgilla kept the embalmed heart of Balliol in a casket after his death in 1268 until her own in 1290. The abbey suffered at the hands of the English in the 13th and 14th centuries, and was dissolved at the Reformation, although 'Roman rites' were practised here until 1610 when the last abbot was ejected.

The church of the abbey with its prominent central tower is particularly well preserved and impressive, while the cloister and domestic buildings have mostly gone except for the chapter house range. There are some old grave slabs, and Devorgilla's rebuilt tomb chest, located in one of the chapels. Much of the massive precinct wall survives, which enclosed an area of some 30 acres.

New Abbey Corn Mill, also in the care of Historic Scotland, is nearby.

Sales area. Disabled access. Joint entry ticket with New Abbey Corn Mill. Parking. £. Combined ticket with New Abbey Corn Mill available (££).

Open Apr-Sep, daily 9.30-18.30; Oct-Mar, Mon-Wed and Sat 9.30-16.30, Thu 9.30-12.00, Sun 14.00-16.30, Fri closed; last entry 30 mins before closing; closed 25/26 Dec and 1/2 Jan.

Tel: 01387 850397

Symington Parish Church

[193 (H4)] Off A77, 3 miles NE of Prestwick, Ayrshire. (NGR: NS 385315 OS: 70)

The fine small parish church dates from 1160 or so, was founded by Simon de Loccard (Lockhart), and retains early features, such as a piscina, lancet windows and an oak-beamed ceiling. It was restored in 1919, and there are fine stained-glass windows. The village is called after Simon Loccard, and the burial ground has interesting markers. Not to be confused with Symington in Lanarkshire, both were founded by Simon (Symington = Simon's town).

Wheelchair access available. Parking nearby.

Open Jul-Aug, Sun 14.00-16.00; other times by appt.

Tel: 01563 830289/205/043 Web: www.symingtonchurch.com

Email: alel@sanderson29.fsnet.co.uk

Tarbat Old Parish Church (Discovery Centre)

[194 (C5)] Off B9165, 8 miles E of Tain, Tarbatness Road, Portmahomack, Highland. (NGR: NH 915845 LR: 21)

The Old Parish Church was rebuilt in 1756 as a T-plan building with an unusual belfry, but retains its original crypt and was dedicated to St Colman. Around the church have been found many Pictish carved stones, and the church has been remodelled as the Discovery Centre. It has displays on one of the largest ongoing archaeological digs in Europe, information on the Picts and a collection of carved stones. There is access to the crypt of the church, and nearby is an old baptismal well.

Explanatory displays. Guided tours of the dig are available when in progress. Audiovisual presentation on the Picts of Easter Ross. Gift shop. Disabled access. Parking. £.

Open Mar-Dec: 1st Sat Mar-1st Sat May, daily 14.00-17.00; 1st Sun May-last Sat Sep, daily 10.00-17.00; last Sun Sep-23 Dec, daily 14.00-17.00; closed 24 Dec-1st Sat Mar.

Tel: 01862 871351   Fax: 01862 871361

Web: www.tarbat-discovery.co.uk   Email: tarbat@globalnet.co.uk

Teampull na Trionaid

[195 (D1)] Off A865, 4 miles NE of Balivanich, Carinish, North Uist. (NGR: NF 816602 LR: 22)

Teampull na Trionaid, Church of The Trinity, dates from the 13th or 14th century, although on an older site, and was one of the largest pre-Reformation churches in the Western Isles. The building is now ruinous, although the small adjoining chapel of Clan MacVicar is better preserved. In 1601 the church was used as a refuge by the MacDonalds from a party of MacLeods from Skye. The MacLeods were routed at the nearby Battle of Carinish.

There was a holy well [NF 814601], known as Tobar na Trionaid.

Parking nearby.

Access at all reasonable times.

Temple Preceptory

[196 (H5)] Off B6372, 3 miles SW of Gorebridge, Temple, Midlothian.
(NGR: NT 315588   LR: 66)

Temple Preceptory was the main seat of the Knights Templar in Scotland, founded by David I in 1175. They were originally established to protect pilgrims in the Holy Land, but they became very powerful throughout Europe, and their order was suppressed in 1312. The property was given to the Knights Hospitaller, who had their base at Torphichen Preceptory (see separate entry).

Set in a picturesque situation below a wooded ridge, little (or nothing) of the Preceptory remains, except the ruined parish church, rectangular in plan with a large gable window. The church dates from the mid 14th century or earlier, and may incorporate, or be built on, the site of the Templar church. The church was repaired in the 1980s, and stands in an interesting burial ground with some notable markers.

Access at all reasonable times.

Torphichen Preceptory (HS) and Kirk

[197 (H5)] Off B792, 4 miles SW of Linlithgow, The Bowyett, West Lothian.
(NGR: NS 972727   LR: 65)

Torphichen Preceptory was the main seat of the Knights Hospitallers (Knights of St John), and was founded by David I in 1153. William Wallace held a convention of barons here in 1298, and Edward I of England stayed here after winning the Battle of Falkirk against Wallace the same year.

A rather unusual and atmospheric building, both inside and out, the lofty crossing and transepts survive with traces of the nave, cloister and other domestic buildings. It dates from the 12th century, but was much altered in the 15th century. There is an exhibition in the upper rooms. The parish church, a T-plan building of 1756, is on the site of the nave. A stone in the burial ground is said to mark the centre of the sanctuary offered by the Preceptory, while other stones, about one mile away, defined the limits (two survive, at Gormyre and Westfield). There are some outstanding burial markers.

Exhibition. Sales area. WC. Car and coach parking. £.

Preceptory and parish church open Apr-Sep, Sat 11.00-17.00, Sun and Bank Hols 14.00-17.00.

Tel: 01506 653475/0131 668 8800

Trumpan Church

[198 (D2)] Off B886, 8 miles NE of Dunvegan, Skye. (NGR: NG 225613   LR: 23)

The atmospheric ruins of a rectangular medieval church, which had a thatched roof and was dedicated to St Conan. The church is the site of a massacre, when the congregation of MacLeods was burned alive by the MacDonalds.

In the old burial ground is the Trial Stone, which has a small hole near the top. If someone succeeded in putting their finger in the hole at the first attempt (while blindfolded) they would be proved to be telling the truth. Lady Grange, imprisoned and carted around the Western Isles after stumbling on her husband's Jacobite plots, is believed to be buried here, and there are also two medieval carved slabs.

Parking Nearby.

Access at all reasonable times.

Tullibardine Chapel (HS)

[199 (G5)] Off A823, 6 miles SE of Crieff, Perthshire. (NGR: NN 909134 LR: 58)

A largely unaltered medieval chapel, cruciform in plan with a small tower at the west end, founded by Sir David Murray of Tullibardine in 1446: it has been used as a burial place by the Murrays since the Reformation. It was dedicated to the Holy Trinity, and was rebuilt about 1500: it is one of the most complete examples of a small collegiate church in Scotland (although it is not clear if the college was actually ever established). It has fine window tracery, heraldic carving and roof.

Exhibition. Parking nearby.

Open Apr-Sep.

Tullich Kirk

[200 (D6)] By A93, 2 miles NE of Ballater, Aberdeenshire. (NGR: NO 390975 LR: 44)

The site is associated with St Nathalan, who died in 678. In railings by one wall are weathered carved stones, including a faint Pictish symbol stone from the 7th century, and other stones with crosses. The ruinous church is rectangular in plan, and stands in a round burial ground with old markers.

Parking.

Access at all reasonable times.

Westside Church (Crosskirk), Westray (HS)

[201 (A6)] Off B9067, 3.5 miles S of Pierowall, Tuquoy, SE side of Westray, Orkney. (NGR: HY 455432 LR: 5)

The ruinous church, dedicated to the Holy Cross, dates from the 12th century, and has a barrel-vaulted chancel. It was founded by the Viking, Hafliki Thorkelsson, and there was a Norse settlement nearby. The church was altered in the 17th century when the nave was enlarged.

Parking nearby.

Access at all reasonable times: walk to site.

Tel: 01856 841815

Whithorn Priory (HS)

[202 (J4)] On A746, Whithorn, Dumfries and Galloway. (NGR: NX 444403 LR: 83)

The site of a monastery of St Ninian, who built a stone church here in the 5th century, dedicated to St Martin of Tours. The church was white washed and known as 'Candida Casa' (white or shining house) and its location was probably within the present ruined priory church. Whithorn was a Anglian bishopric but is last mentioned in 803. St Ninian was active in converting the Britons of Galloway, and also made missions to the north.

Nothing definite remains from this period, except carved stones.

Whithorn was a popular place of pilgrimage in medieval times, and attracted 1000s of pilgrims, both from Scotland, England, Ireland and elsewhere. Robert the Bruce, David II and James III, IV and V all made their way here, and Mary, Queen of Scots, visited in 1563. The arm bone of St Ninian was taken to the Scottish seminary at Douai after the Reformation, where it was kept until the French Revolution.

The existing ruins are of a 12th-century Premonstratensian priory and cathedral: only the nave of what was a large Romanesque church survives, although it is unroofed. The subterranean vaulted chambers were probably used to house the shrine and relics of St Ninian.

Part of the church continued to be used as a cathedral and parish church after the Reformation, even after the western tower had collapsed, and was not abandoned until 1822 when the nearby modern church (St Ninian's Priory Church) was built on the site of the east cloister. This church has a later tower, a carved oak pulpit and stained glass windows.

A fine collection of early Christian sculpture is housed in the nearby Whithorn: Cradle of Christianity in Scotland, including the Latinus Stone, the earliest Christian memorial in Scotland; the St Peter's Stone; and the 10th-century Monreith Cross, which is carved with interlaced patterns and has a round head. The discovery centre features guided tours of the excavations of an abandoned town near the priory, the priory itself, the museum and crypts, as well as an audiovisual presentation.

Explanatory boards. Disabled access. Parking nearby. Joint ticket with Whithorn Priory and Museum £ (priory, priory museum and archaeological dig).

Open Easter-Oct, daily 10.30-17.00 – tel to confirm;
St Ninian's Priory Church, open Easter-Oct 10.00-17.00.
Tel: 01988 500508

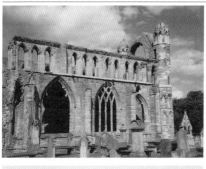

Top left: Elgin Cathedral   Above left: St Vigeans Church
Above right: Sueno's Stone, Forres
Bottom left: Kincardine O'Neil Old Church   Bottom right: Whithorn Priory

Saints

Some of the more popular or interesting saints associated with Scotland or mentioned in the text are listed below, although the list is not intended to be exhaustive: there were a great many saints, both native and international. As there are few records of the time, many of these individuals remain shadowy, and others no doubt benefited from the invention of later writers. There was also a desire by the church (and Crown) to show an unbroken line of saints (and kings) through Ireland, from where the Scots had originated. This may have led to the emphasis on Columba, and his contemporaries, as the main missionaries to Scotland, rather than the earlier Ninian and Palladius and their followers, who were either British, Pictish or foreign. This may have also contributed to dates being altered to suit this later chronology. Where possible, the saints have been related back to the sites in the text. Dates may be very approximate.

Andrew (c. 60) Patron saint of Scotland (and Greece, Romania and Russia). Andrew has no direct connection with Scotland. He was active in Scythia, and then martyred on an 'X' shaped cross at Patras. His relics were kept at Constantinople, then Amalfi, and some of them are said to have been brought to Scotland by Rule (after a shipwreck) and kept at St Andrews (then known as Kilrymont). Alternatively they were brought here in 733 by Acca, Bishop of Hexham. The Rule version is likely to be suspect: a later fabrication to provide a long history for the Scottish church and its connection with Andrew.

 The flag of Scotland, the saltire (a white cross on a blue background), represents St Andrew's crucifixion. One story is that the cross appeared in the sky before a victory over the Northumbrians, and this was attributed to the saint's intercession. There were numerous dedications (or rededications) to the saint. Festival day: 30 November.

Angus Angus studied at Dunblane and was active in the Balquhidder area, which he believed was so beautiful as to be nearer heaven than other places. He was buried at Balquhidder, and St Angus's Stone may have marked his burial. His day is celebrated on the 2nd Wednesday in August.

Baldred (d. 608? or d. 756?) Baldred is said to have been a follower of Mungo, but his death is given as either 608 or 756. He was active in East Lothian, and when he died three corpses are said to have appeared so that three churches could have the privilege of burying him. Festival day: 6 March.

Bathan/Baithene/Bothan/Bean? (536-600?) Bathan succeeded his cousin, Columba, as abbot of Iona. He is associated with Tiree, and died about 600, on the same day of the year as Columba. He is said to be buried in St Oran's

Chapel on Iona, and Abbey St Bathans is called after him. There is also a dedication at Bowden (Bothanden). Festival day: 9 June.

Bean (d. 1012) Bean was Bishop of Mortlach in Moray in the 10th or 11th century. The dedication at Fowlis Wester is to Bean. Festival day: 16 December.

Blane/Blaan (c. 565-c. 630) Blane is said to have been born on Bute, where he is said to have been instructed by his uncle Catan, and is associated with Dunblane, where he founded a church (in 602?). He made missions into both southern and central Scotland, including the Picts, and northern England, and is believed to be buried at Kingarth. Festival day: 11 August.

Brendan (of Clonfert)/Birnie (484-577) Brendan (the Navigator), from Ireland, made missions up the Western seaboard of Scotland, and probably through the Pentland Firth and then down the east coast – as well as much greater journeys: to Iceland, Greenland and even America. There are many dedications to him, such as at Kilbrannan, Birnie Kirk, and Auld Kirk of Kilbirnie. He is also associated with Eileach an Naoimh. Festival day: 16 May.

Bride/Bridget/Brigit (452?-525?) Bride or Bridget was a saint from Ireland, although Brigit is also a goddess in Celtic mythology, associated with regrowth and rebirth. There were many dedications to her, including at Dalgety, Abernethy, Bothwell and Douglas. Festival day: 1 February.

Brioc (d. 510?) Brioc is said to have lived in the 5th or 6th century, and there were dedications at Rothesay and Montrose, as well as in Wales, Cornwall and Brittany. Festival day: 29-30 April.

Catan/Cattan/Chattan Catan was from Ireland, and founded a monastery at Kingarth on Bute, where he instructed his nephew Blane. He was kinsmen to Comgall of the famous abbey of Bangor, and is commemorated in the names Ardchattan, and Kildalton, where there was probably an early monastery.

Colman (605-76) There are many Irish saints with this name. The most famous in Scotland was a monk from Iona who followed Finian as abbot of Lindisfarne. He led the Celtic party at the Synod of Whitby, although he lost the debate and withdrew to Iona. There are dedications to Colman at Inchmahome in Stirlingshire and Tarbat in Easter Ross. Festival day: 8 August.

Columba/Colmkille (c. 521-597) Columba was born in Donegal in 521, and established a monastic community on Iona in 563. He made a mission to the northern Picts of mainland Scotland, ruled by Brude. Near Inverness, Columba had a trial of power with one of the king's magi at Loch Ness. Indeed, the first account of a creature in Loch Ness is also related at this time, as Columba is said to have saved a servant from the monster. Columba died in 597 at Iona, but was lucky enough to have a dedicated biographer, Adamnan. There were dedications at Dunkeld, Cramond, Largs Old Kirk, Oronsay, Aignish, and the abbey of Inchcolm. St Columba's Cave at Ellary is also associated with the saint. Festival day: 9 June.

Conan/Mochonog (d. 648?) Patron saint of Lorne. Conan was from Ireland, spent time on Iona, and became the Bishop of Man. He is associated with the area around Glenorchy and Dalmally, and St Vigeans. There are dedications at Lochawe (albeit modern) and Trumpan on Skye. Festival day: 26 January.

Congan/Cowan/Congal Congan was brought up in Ireland around the turn of the 8th century, but travelled to Scotland where he was active among the Picts. He was abbot of a monastery at Turriff, and was uncle of St Fillan. In about 1600, following the Reformation, a large wooden statue of the saint was taken to Edinburgh and there burnt in an attempt to stamp out idolatry. Festival day: 13 October.

Constantine (of Cornwall/Scotland) (d. 598) Constantine is said to have been a king of Brittany, and to have led a less than saintly life until the death of his wife when he saw the error of his ways. He came from Cornwall to Scotland, where he established a monastery at Govan: his relics were kept here. He appears to have been a friend of Mirren from Paisley, and was (unusually for Scotland) martyred in Kintyre. He was attacked and his arm severed: he bled to death. Festival day: 11 March.

Conval (d. 612?) Conval was from Ireland, and is said to have been a colleague of Mungo at Glasgow. He was active in Renfrew, and is believed to have established a monastery at Inchinnan. Festival day: 28 September.

Cormac Cormac was a contemporary of Brendan and Columba, and is associated with Eilean Mor, a small island off Argyll, where he is said to be buried, as well as also Keills, south of Tayvallich. Festival day: 14 September?

Curitan (Curdy)/Boniface/Kyrin/Kiritinus Curitan, also known as Boniface was born in Rome, and involved in the reorganisation of the Pictish church in the 8th century to the Roman form of worship. He settled at Rosemarkie, where he died and was buried. Many churches associated with the saint were dedicated to St Peter, such as at Rosemarkie/Fortrose, Aberlemno, and Meigle, although they may have previously had native saint dedications (Rosemarkie was founded by Moluag). The original foundation of Restenneth Priory is said to have been by Curitan in 710. Festival day: 14 March.

Cuthbert (634-687) Cuthbert was born in the Borders, where he was a shepherd. He was taught at the monastery at Old Melrose, before going to Lindisfarne in 685 and the Farne Islands. His relics were eventually translated to Durham Cathedral. There were many dedications to Cuthbert, including at Kirkcudbright, Dalmeny, Coldingham, and in Edinburgh (and hence the name of the Co-op: St Cuthberts). Festival day: 20 March.

Devenick/Demhan Devenick is associated with the north-east of Scotland, but little else is known about him, except that he is supposed to be buried at Creich, where there is the 9th- or 10th-century St Demhan's Cross. Banchory Devenick is called after him.

Donan/Donnan (d. 618?) Donan was a contemporary of Columba and came from Ireland. He founded a monastery on the island of Eigg, and there (unusually for Scotland) was slain along with his followers, although who the murders were is unclear. There are many dedications to the saint, usually as Kildonan, and Eilean Donan Castle is called after him. Festival day: 16/17 August.

Drostan/Dunstan/Dustan/Modrustus Although Drostan is said to have been a follower, even nephew, of Columba, it is possible that he was a Pictish saint. He is associated with Deer, Canisbay and the north-east of Scotland, and is named on one of the stones in St Vigean's Museum. There are other dedications in Fife and Galloway. Festival day: 11 July.

Duthac/Duthus/Dutho (1000?-1065?) Duthac was said to have been born in Tain about 1000 at the site of St Duthac's Chapel. Duthac was a great scholar and may have died in Ireland about 1065, but his relics were translated to Tain (although not until 1253?), which became a place of pilgrimage. His shirt was said to protect the wearer from death, although it did the Earl of Ross no good at all at Halidon Hill in 1333: the earl was slain. The English kindly returned the shirt. Festival day: 8 March.

Ebba/Abb (d. 683 or 679?) Ebba, daughter of Ethelfrith of Northumbria, founded a monastery near St Abb's in the 7th century, and died around 683. The monastery was later burned, and eventually refounded at Coldingham. A more dramatic version is that Ebba was slain by Norsemen, although this is recorded as in 870 and may be an elaboration or confusion with a later abbess, who may also have been called Ebba. Festival day: 25 August or 2 April.

Enoch/Thenew/Denw/Thanay Enoch or Thenew was a daughter of the king of Lothian, fell pregnant although unmarried, and her father tried to have her killed by throwing her off Traprain Law, although she survived unhurt. She was then cast adrift at the Isle of May, but found her way up the Forth to Culross, aided by a shoal of fish, where she was taken in by Serf. She had a son, Mungo (Kentigern). Enoch had a church in Glasgow, commemorated by the railway station, square and shopping centre. Festival day: 18 July.

Erchan Erchan is associated with Kincardine O'Neil.

Fergus Fergus is said to have been a nephew of Columba, but it is possible that he was an earlier Pictish saint, although a Fergus, Scottish Bishop of Picts, was in Rome in 721. Fergus was active in Angus and Caithness, and is associated with Glamis, where most of him is said to be buried: his head ended up at

Scone Abbey, a neck bone and joint at St Andrews Cathedral, and one of his arms at Aberdeen: there was money to be made from relics. The fair at Glamis continued to be held on 18 November, and there was another dedication to him at Eassie. The village of St Fergus is also named after him. Festival day: 27 or 18 November.

Fiacre/Fiachrach/Fevre (d. 670?) Fiacre was raised in a monastery in Ireland in the 7th century, but went to France where he became renowned as a great gardener, herbalist and healer. There was a dedication at Nigg. Festival day: 30 Aug/1 Sep?

Fillan There is more than one saint with this name: one Fillan, a leper, was active in the 6th century, while a later Fillan is said to have died around 777, and was the nephew of Comgall of Turriff. This Fillan is associated with the area around Glendochart, and the top of his crosier is preserved in the Museum of Scotland, while his bell was associated with cures. Those with mental illness were immersed in the pool of Strathfillan, then left bound overnight: if they were free in the morning they were freed. Many miracles were associated with him, including taming a wolf using only the power of prayer. Robert the Bruce carried his relics at the Battle of Bannockburn in 1314. There are numerous dedications to Fillan, including at Aberdour, and in Argyll and in Galloway, and a cave associated with him at Pittenweem. There is information about Fillan at the Breadalbane Folklore Centre. Festival days: 22 June; 9 or 19 January.

Finbar/Barr/Finian/Winning/Winian (d. 579?) Again there is more than one saint with this name. Also known as Finian of Moville, from a monastery he founded in Ireland, Finian was associated with Whithorn in the 6th century, and was a renowned scholar, active in many parts of Scotland. Chapel Finian, near Mochrum, was dedicated to him. Kilwinning, with the remains of the medieval abbey, was also named after him.

The people of Barra are said to have been converted to Christianity (and away from cannibalism) by Barr or Finbar of Cork: the island is named after him. Barr is said to have crossed the sea on horseback, and the sun did not set on Cloyne in Ireland for two weeks after his death there in 610-630? Festival days: 10 September; 25 September.

Gilbert (d. 1246) Gilbert de Moravia was Bishop of Caithness from 1233-46, and founded Dornoch Cathedral. Gilbert was made a saint, and is buried in the cathedral.

Giles/Egidius/Aegidius (d. 725) Giles was born in Greece, but moved to France and there became a monk. Many miracles were attributed to him, and he established a monastery at Arles. There was a church dedicated to him in

Edinburgh by the 12th century. His festival day was celebrated by a parade of his statue and a relic, his arm bone encased in silver. In 1558 there was a riot and the statue was destroyed. There was also a dedication to Giles in Elgin. Festival day: 1 September.

John There are many dedications to both John the Baptist and John the Evangelist, although it is not always clear to whom.

John the Baptist foretold the coming of Christ, and was executed, beheaded and martyred, sometime around 30 AD following Salome's dancing. His festival day was midsummer's day, and was associated with rituals for securing a good harvest. St John's Wort was gathered to protect against evil, and Ayr, Perth, Dalry and Corstorphine had dedications to him. The Knights of St John (Knights Hospitallers) had their preceptory at Torphichen. Festival day: 24 June.

John the Evangelist wrote one of the four gospels and a description of the apocalypse as described in Revelations. He died in about 100, and there were dedications all over Scotland. Festival day: 27 December.

Kenneth/Cainnech (c. 525-c. 600) Kenneth (or Cainnech) of Aghaboe, was a contemporary of Columba, Brendan and Cormac, and studied in Ireland, before going to Wales. He came to Scotland, but eventually returned to his monastery at Aghaboe, where he died. There are many dedications to him, including Inchkenneth, an island off Mull. Festival day: 11 October.

Machar/Mochonnon (c. 600) Machar is believed have been born in Ireland and to have been one of the 12 followers of Columba, but he may have been an a Pictish saint, as he was said to have been contemporary with Ternan. He made a mission to the north-east, and founded at church at what is now St Machar's Cathedral in Old Aberdeen. Machar became bishop of Tours, where he died. Festival day: 12 November.

Machute/Maclou/Malo (c. 520-c. 620) Maclou or Machute was born in England or south-west Wales, and was a follower of Brendan. He accompanied Brendan on his voyages up the west coast of Scotland, and was active in Orkney. He settled in France in the St Malo area, which is called after him. A relic of his, encased in gold, was held at the priory at Lesmahagow, which is also called after him. Festival day: 15 November.

Maelrubha (c. 642-722) Maelrubha came to Scotland from Bangor in Ireland in 671, and founded a monastery at Applecross, from where he made many missions to the north. The saint died in 722, and is said to be buried at Applecross: earth taken from his grave before setting out on a journey would ensure a safe return. He became associated with the Celtic god Mourie and rituals involving the sacrifice of bulls, divination and healing. There are many dedications, including Applecross, Isle Maree in Loch Maree, and Balnakeil in Sutherland. Festival day: 21 April or 22 August.

Magnus (1117?) Magnus the Martyr, grandson to Thorfinn the Mighty and Earl of Orkney, is said to have been a pious and gentle man (at least for a Norseman), and was murdered in 1117 on the order of his cousin Earl Haakon, so that Haakon might rule Orkney by himself. Following miracles attributed to his relics, then interred at Birsay, Magnus's fame spread, and there are churches dedicated to him in the Faroes, Iceland and London. His relics were taken from Birsay to St Magnus Cathedral in Kirkwall. Egilsay is said to have been the site of his execution. Festival day: 16 April.

Margaret (1046?-93) Granddaughter of Edmund Ironside, King of England, and wife of Malcolm Canmore, Malcolm III of Scots, she came to Scotland after the defeat at the Battle of Hastings. Margaret was a good and pious woman, and mother to the Kings Edgar, Alexander I and David I. She also benefited from her devoted biographer Turgot. Margaret and Malcolm were buried in Dunfermline Abbey, although their remains were taken to the Continent at the Reformation. There is also a cave associated with her in Dunfermline. A small chapel in Edinburgh Castle is dedicated to her, while her Gospel Book is in the Bodleian Library at Oxford. Festival day: 16 November.

Marnon/Marnock/Marny/Ernene/Mernog Marnock was born in Ireland and educated there, before coming to Scotland, where he is said to have died at Aberchirder. Here, it is recorded, his skull was washed and the water used to cure the sick and infirm. Fowlis Easter Church is dedicated to him, and he gave his name to Kilmarnock. Festival day: 25 October or 18 August.

Martin of Tours (c. 335-c. 415) Martin was born in Hungary in the 4th century, and served in the Roman army: one story concerning him is that he gave half his cloak to a freezing beggar. He became bishop of Tours, and there were many dedications in France and elsewhere. Whithorn may have originally been dedicated to him, as was Kilmartin. Festival day: 11 November.

Mary/Blessed Virgin/Our Lady Mother of God, giving her a unique place, having given birth to Jesus. By far the most dedications to any saint in Scotland, although they are generally thought to be from around or after the 10th century, rather than from earlier times. Festival days: several.

Mary Magdalene Mary Magdalene was revered as an archetypal repentant sinner, and was the first to see Christ after the Resurrection. Magdalen Chapel in Edinburgh was dedicated to her. Festival day: 22 July.

Matthew One of Jesus's disciples, Matthew wrote the first Gospel, and had worked as a tax collector until he followed Christ. Rosslyn Chapel was dedicated to him. Festival day: 21 September.

Michael One of the archangels, a supernatural being, to whom many dedications (often with the addition of All Saints) were made in early Christian times, including at Kinkell and Linlithgow. His day, Michaelmas, was a major celebration and festival. Festival day: 29 September.

Mirren Mirren is said to have come from Bangor in Ireland in the 6th century, and to have settled at Paisley, where he founded a monastery about 560. He was a contemporary of Constantine. Paisley Abbey is dedicated to Mirren, and the local football team named after him; as is Inchmurrin, an island in Loch Lomond. Festival day: 15 September.

Modan Modan was born in the Highlands in the 6th or 7th century, and is said to have founded a church at Falkirk, and to have died at Rosneath near Dumbarton. He may have been a contemporary of Ronan, and is also associated with Ardchattan. Festival day: 4 February.

Molaise/Molios/Laisren Molaise was St Blane's nephew, and may have been educated at the monastery at Kingarth on Bute. His is associated with Lamlash and Arran and the Holy Island there (now a Buddhist retreat) Festival day: 18 April.

Moluag/Moluoc/Lugaidn (d. 592) Moluag studied at Bangor in Ireland, and is associated with Lismore, where he founded a monastery. According to legend, he was determined to reach Lismore before Columba, who was approaching the island ahead of Moluag. So much so, that Moluag cut off his little finger and threw it onto the island so that he could claim possession as having 'touched' land first. He died at Rosemarkie, but his relics were brought back to Lismore: his crosier is still kept at Bachuil. There were dedications to him in many parts of Scotland, including Eoropie on Lewis, Rosemarkie, Mortlach, and Crail. Festival day: 4 August.

Monan (d. 870?) Monan was a monk at St Andrews, and is associated with St Monans in Fife. He was reputedly slain by Norsemen in about 870, and St Monans held his relics. Festival day: 1 March.

Monirus (d. 824?) Monirus was active around Balvenie, and is associated with Crathie. Festival day: 18 December.

Mungo/Kentigern (c. 518-c. 603) Mungo (or more properly Kentigern, Mungo means 'dear friend') was the son of Enoch (Thenew), and was educated by Serf at Culross. Mungo was active among the Britons of Strathclyde and founded a church at Glasgow, on the site of which stands the cathedral. He performed many miracles, and one story is that Mungo helped an unfaithful queen recover a ring thrown into the sea by the king. If she did not find it in three days, she was to be executed. Mungo prayed with the woman, and a salmon caught by one of Mungo's followers had swallowed the ring. The ring and the salmon form the basis of Glasgow's coat of arms. There are many dedications, including at Borthwick, Crichton and Stobo. Festival day: 14 January.

Munn/Fintan Munnu Munn, was a contemporary and cousin of Columba, and joined him on Iona, although he returned to Ireland and there founded a great monastery. He is said to have suffered from leprosy, and is associated with Kilmun and other sites in Argyll. Festival day: 21 October.

Nathalan (d. 678) Nathalan is associated with Tullich in Aberdeenshire, where he spent his youth and founded a church. He made a pilgrimage to Rome, but was buried at Tullich. Festival day: 8 January.

Nicholas Nicholas lived in the 4th century, was revered as a protector of children and the defenceless, and has become linked to Santa Claus. Dedications to him include Biggar, Cross Kirk at Peebles, Orphir on Orkney, at Dalkeith, and Kirk of St Nicholas in Aberdeen. Festival day: 6 December.

Ninian/Ringan (c.360-c. 432) Ninian is the first named saint to bring Christianity to Scotland. A Briton, said to have been educated in Rome, he founded a religious community at Whithorn by 430, known as *Candida Casa* (white house), where he was bishop. Physgill and Isle of Whithorn are also associated with him. Ninian made missions north to the Picts and the Britons of Strathclyde, and there are dedications all over Scotland. Festival day: 16 September or 26 August.

Palladius/Paldy (c. 432) Palladius made a mission to Scotland, having been sent to the north by Pope Celestine in 431, and reputedly instructed other saints, such as Serf and Ternan. Palladius is commemorated in place names in the Mearns, Dunning, Glen Lyon and Fordoun (St Paldy), where he is said to have died. Festival day: 7 July.

Patrick (c. 389-c. 461) Patron saint and Apostle of Ireland. Patrick was born in Britain, possibly at Kilpatrick near Dumbarton, although it is a matter of some debate. Patrick was seized and sold into slavery in Ireland, although he eventually escaped. During his captivity, he was filled with a zeal for spreading the word. He is credited with bringing Christianity to Ireland, based in Saul in County Down, where he died, as well as expelling the snakes from Ireland. There are many dedications to Patrick in Scotland, including Muthill. Festival day: 17 March.

Peter First of the Apostles, first Pope, and the gatekeeper of heaven. There are many dedications to Peter in Scotland, including Aberlemno, Fortrose, Restenneth, Duffus and Thurso. These early dedications are often associated with Curitan. Festival day: 29 June.

Queran/Kiaran (c. 516-c. 556) An early apostle in Ireland, it is not clear if he visited Scotland; or possibly a 9th-century Scottish saint. Probably associated with the well at Islesteps near Dumfries, there was also a dedication at Kilchoman on Islay. Festival day: 9 September.

Ronan Ronan is recorded as being at the Synod of Whitby, and is associated with Rona, an island north of Lewis, and St Ronan's Wells at Innerleithen. He may have been a friend of Modan. Festival day: 7 February or 1 June.

Rule/Regulus Rule was active around St Andrews in Fife at the beginning of the Christian period, although little is known about him and a date of the 4th century seems somewhat early. He is attributed with bringing the relics of St Andrew to Scotland, but this is likely to be no more than a legend, and Acca, Bishop of Hexham, is usually credited. St Rule's Tower, by the remains of St Andrews Cathedral, is from a church dedicated to Rule, and Crossraguel is said to be called after him. Festival day: 17 October or 30 March.

Serf/Servanus (d. 583?) An early saint, who may have been instructed by Palladius, is credited with taking in the pregnant Enoch (Thenew), and instructing her son Mungo (Kentigern) at Culross. Serf is also said to have slain a 'fell dragon'. He is associated with one of the islands in Loch Leven, site of a later priory, and there are dedications at Abercorn, Dunning, Logie Old Kirk, Tullibody and around the Ochils. Festival day: 1 July.

Ternan (d. 431?) Ternan was born in Arbuthnott, probably in the 5th century, and is said to have been a disciple of Palladius. He may have been abbot of Whithorn, and is believed to have died at Banchory. The churches at Abuthnott and Banchory were dedicated to him. Festival day: 12 June.

Thomas the Martyr Thomas a Becket, Archbishop of Canterbury, was murdered on the orders of King Henry of England. He had been a friend of William I King of Scots, who dedicated Arbroath Abbey to Thomas after being released from imprisonment in England. Festival day: 29 December.

Triduana/Trodwin/Tredwell Triduana is said to have arrived in Scotland with Rule (or Curitan). She was a good-looking Greek girl, desired by the pagan Nechtan, who admired her beautiful eyes. So, she took her own eyes out and gave them to Nechtan on a thorn when he pursued her. There are parallels for this story in both Ireland and the Continent, so the truth of it is questionable. Triduana is associated with Rescobie in Angus and Restalrig near Edinburgh, although there are other dedications in Scotland. Visiting her shrines was believed to help illnesses and problems of the eye, including blindness. Festival day: 9 November.

Vigean/Fechin (d. 664) Vigean or Fechin was from Ireland, and it is not clear if he visited Scotland. There are dedications to him at St Vigeans near Arbroath and at Ecclefechan. Festival day: 20 January.

Orders

MONASTIC ORDERS

Celtic monasticism – introduced at Iona by Irish monks from the 6th century. Essentially hermits who lived isolated, ascetic lives in individual cells located around a communal oratory.

Benedictine Order – founded about 530 at Monte Cassino, by St Benedictine of Nursia. Much later a united network of abbeys was created. Seven Benedictine abbeys founded in Scotland, of which Dunfermline was the most important.

Cluniac Order – reformed order of Benedictines. Attempted to re-establish a stricter form of monasticism. Abbey founded at Cluny, France in 909 and later formed a separate order of monasteries. Three Cluniac houses founded in Scotland. Both the worship and the buildings of this order would eventually become extremely elaborate, despite their initial attempts at simplicity. Crossraguel, a Cluniac abbey, was founded in 1214 by Duncan, Earl of Carrick.

Tironensian Order – founded in France by St Bernard of Tiron in 1109 as a reformed Benedictine order. First foundation in Scotland, and Britain, was at Selkirk, in 1113 by David I. Later the order moved to Kelso, and a further seven houses were established throughout Scotland. Arbroath is the best surviving example of a Tironensian abbey, although Kelso was larger and wealthier.

Cistercian Order – another reformed Benedictine order. Founded by St Robert of Molesme at Cîteaux in France, in 1098. St Bernard insisted that the monastic buildings should be plain and built away from towns and population settlements. Introduced, also by David I, at Melrose in 1136. Later 12 abbeys established in Scotland. Melrose and Sweetheart are the two best surviving examples.

Valliscaulian Order – reformed order, although formed much later. Mother house was at Val de Choux, in France, and first reached Scotland in 1230. Three Scottish priories founded: Ardchattan, Beauly and Pluscarden, although the latter has been restored and is now a Benedictine abbey.

ORDERS OF CANONS

Augustinian Canons – earliest house founded at Scone in 1120 by Alexander I. Later about 18 houses established. The abbeys of Inchcolm and Jedburgh and the priory at Inchmahome, are all interesting examples of Augustinian houses.

Premonstratensian Canons – founded in France by St Norbert of Xanten, at Prémontré, in 1120. Ascetic order of canons, similar to Cistercian order of monks. Likely to have been introduced at Dryburgh, and a further five houses were founded in Scotland. Both Dryburgh Abbey and the priory at Whithorn have substantial remains.

Trinitarian Canons – had eight houses in Scotland. At the Cross Kirk in Peebles are the ruins and foundations of the Trinitarian priory founded in 1474, the only surviving house of this order.

ORDERS OF FRIARS

Dominican Friars – known as Blackfriars, established by St Dominic at Toulouse, France, in 1215. First reached Scotland in 1230.

Franciscan Friars – known as Greyfriars, were established by St Francis in 1215. Reached Scotland about 1231. Both orders became linked with the newly formed universities which appeared in Europe in the 13th century.

ORDERS OF KNIGHTS

Knights Hospitallers – or Knights of the Hospital of St John of Jerusalem, founded in the 12th century to provide care for sick and poor, and to provide safe escort to the Holy Land. They followed the Augustinian order and were introduced to Scotland by David I about 1144. The preceptory at Torphichen was the Scottish headquarters of the order.

Knights Templars – another military order also introduced by David I. In 1312 the order was suppressed by the Pope and their property passed to the Knights Hospitallers. Although there was a preceptory at Temple, little or nothing remains of the original buildings.

Glossary

Abbey Monastery headed by an abbot

Abbot Head of abbey of monks or canons

Aisle Outer part of body of church, separated by an arcade of pillars

Apse Semi circular or polygonal east end of church, contained altar

Arcade Row of arches

Aumbry Recess for storing books, vessels

Bishop Head of church diocese

Calefactory The warming house, only heated room in monasteries

Campanile Bell-tower

Canon Member of order of priests serving cathedral or abbey

Carillon Set of bells (for playing tunes)

Chancel Eastern end of church used by clergy and choir

Chapterhouse Used to discuss monastic business; burial place of abbots

Chevrons Zig-zag carving, feature of Romanesque architecture

Choir Part of chancel used by priests and singers; also spelt quire

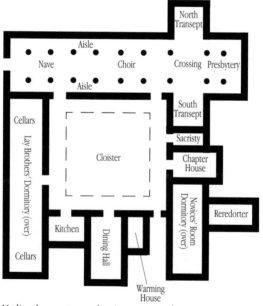

Medieval monastery – showing common elements

Cinquefoil	Cusped decoration, divides arch or circle into five parts
Clerestory	Upper windows over aisles
Cloister	Rectangular area around which monastic buildings were placed
Collegiate church	Church with college of priests to pray for the dead
Commendator	Person holding revenues of abbey; not always a churchman
Crossing	Part of church where nave, chancel and transepts intersect
Cruciform church	Cross-shaped church, transepts form shape of cross
Crypt	Basement area, often vaulted, sometimes used for burials
Day stair	To the dormitory from the cloister, used during the day
Diocese	Area served by cathedral and bishop
Dormitory or dorter	Sleeping accommodation
Effigy	Bronze or stone figure on tomb, usually horizontal or recumbent
Font	Ceremonial baptism basin
Frater	Monastic dining area or refectory
Friars	Religious brothers, bound by vows, not confined to monasteries
Gargoyle	Ornate water spout
Gothic	Pointed-arch style of architecture, introduced mid 12th century
Infirmary	Building where the sick were cared for
Kirk	Church (Scotland)
Lavatorium	Washing area
Lectern	Reading desk
Manse	Minister's house
Misericord	Ledge found in stalls, used to rest by older or infirm clergy, during long periods of standing. Often highly decorated
Monastery	Buildings housing a community of monks, canons or nuns
Nave	Area of church where the lay congregation stood
Night stair	From the dormitory to church, used for night services
Norman	See Romanesque
Parlour	Room where monks were permitted to talk
Piscina	Basin in wall, used to wash communion vessels
Precinct	The grounds around monastery, enclosed by boundary wall
Presbytery	East part of church; the priest's quarters; or post-Reformation level of church administration between kirk and synod
Priory	Monastery headed by a prior, less important than an abbey
Reformation	Rejection of the authority of Rome by Protestants
Reredos	Screen or wall decoration at the back of an altar
Reredorter	Latrine block connected to dormitory
Romanesque	Round-arched style of architecture c. 11th/12th centuries
Rood	Crucifix, cross
Rood screen	Screen between chancel and nave, often carved, separating clergy from congregation
Sacrament house	Ornate cupboard for storing sacrament

Glossary

Sacristy	Room where sacred vessels and vestments stored (vestry)
Sedilia	Seats in the chancel, usually in threes, for priests
Shrine	Contained saint's body or relics
Slype	Passage out of cloister
Stalls	Seats for singers or dignitaries
Stoup	Basin for holy water, found at entrance to church
Teinds	Tenth part of household goods, paid to the church in kind
Tracery	Intersected rib work found in later Gothic windows
Trefoil	Three-lobed decoration
Undercroft	Basement or crypt

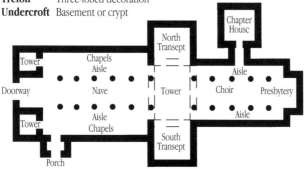

Medieval cathedral – showing common elements

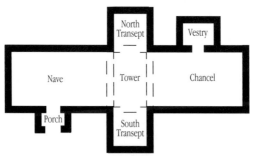

Collegiate church – showing common elements

Medieval parish church – showing common elements

Index

Index

Index